Dictionaries: A Very Short Introduction

VERY SHORT INTRODUCTIONS are for anyone wanting a stimulating and accessible way into a new subject. They are written by experts, and have been translated into more than 45 different languages.

The series began in 1995, and now covers a wide variety of topics in every discipline. The VSI library now contains over 500 volumes—a Very Short Introduction to everything from Psychology and Philosophy of Science to American History and Relativity—and continues to grow in every subject area.

Titles in the series include the following:

Lynda Mugglestone

DICTIONARIES

A Very Short Introduction

OXFORD
UNIVERSITY PRESS

OXFORD

UNIVERSITY PRESS

Great Clarendon Street, Oxford ox2 6DP

Oxford University Press is a department of the University of Oxford.
It furthers the University's objective of excellence in research, scholarship,
and education by publishing worldwide in

Oxford New York

Auckland Cape Town Dar es Salaam Hong Kong Karachi
Kuala Lumpur Madrid Melbourne Mexico City Nairobi
New Delhi Shanghai Taipei Toronto

With offices in

Argentina Austria Brazil Chile Czech Republic France Greece
Guatemala Hungary Italy Japan Poland Portugal Singapore
South Korea Switzerland Thailand Turkey Ukraine Vietnam

Oxford is a registered trade mark of Oxford University Press
in the UK and in certain other countries

Published in the United States
by Oxford University Press Inc., New York

First published 2011

British Library Cataloguing in Publication Data
Data available

Library of Congress Cataloging in Publication Data
Data available

Typeset by SPI Publisher Services, Pondicherry, India
Printed in Great Britain
on acid-free paper by
CPI Group (UK) Ltd, Croydon, CR0 4YY

ISBN 978-0-19-957379-0

7 9 10 8 6

Contents

Preface

'A large work is difficult because it is large', wrote Samuel Johnson, one of the most famous of dictionary-makers, in the Preface to his *Dictionary of the English Language* which he published in 1755. Writing a *Very Short Introduction* to dictionaries prompts a rather different conclusion – that 'A very short book is very difficult because it is particularly short'. Even Johnson found he could not include all that he had originally intended ('such is design, while it is yet at a distance from execution', as he lamented). Similar problems have, all too often, confronted attempts to encompass the complexity and diversity of dictionaries within a single volume – not least, of course, since the history and use of dictionaries spans over 4,000 years. Execution, rather than design, has meant, for instance, that thesauruses have had to be cast aside and the focus on regional and slang lexicography often reduced, along with other interesting domains of use from children's dictionaries to the sheer range of bilingual and polyglot dictionaries across the world.

In some ways, of course, one could nevertheless wonder why we need a *Very Short Introduction* to Dictionaries at all. The very familiarity of dictionaries – there are, surveys suggest, few homes in which a dictionary is not present in some shape or form – mean that the dictionary as text is often strikingly taken for granted. Familiarity in this sense often renders the modern dictionary a literally unremarkable presence. Not to our credit, we can assume that the dictionary simply exists, an impassive – and entirely neutral – repository of information. We habitually forget to consider, say, the countless acts of selection and choice by which any dictionary is, in reality, brought into being. Such assumptions will often find themselves under scrutiny here. Dictionaries, as this volume will explore, are far more than works that list the words and meanings of a language or languages. All dictionaries are partial, and all are selective. The kind of selections made, and the choices that underpin the making of any single dictionary, are the diverse narratives which instead lie behind the neatly printed pages of the finished text.

Dictionaries, seen in this light, are often all too human products, able to reflect the social and cultural assumptions of the time in which they are written, and telling, as a result, their own stories of society, culture, innovation, and ideals. Who writes a dictionary – and when and where – are factors which, in significant ways, will change and influence the kind of dictionary that is produced. Chapters within this book engage thematically with the nature and identity of dictionaries, and with the diverse realities of dictionary-making, whether in manuscript or in the modern digital age. Common beliefs about dictionaries are often put to the test, as in Chapters 4 and 5 which tackle the topics of authority and truth. Chapter 6 explores the challenges faced by modern dictionary-making, not least in the ways in which the Internet can seem to offer the opportunity for everyone to be a dictionary-maker should they so wish. While this volume provides an overview of relevant areas, further reading, included at the end of the volume, offers other directions that can productively be explored.

Acknowledgements

Acknowledgements are due to the Bodleian Library, University of Oxford, for permission to reproduce the image of Samuel Johnson's annotations to Robert Burton's *Anatomy of Melancholy* (1676) (Dep. c. 25/1), and also for permission to reproduce the image in Chapter 6 from Joseph Wright's annotated notebooks of the *English Dialect Dictionary* (MS. Eng. Lang. d. 78). I would also like to acknowledge the help of Penny Silva at the Oxford English Dictionary, Beverley Hunt in the Oxford University Press archives, and Joanna Rubery from Oxford Language Dictionaries, as well as the many other people who have offered information and advice during the making of this volume.

List of illustrations

Chapter 1
Identity

'You are to write it,' said the Earl.

'I!' exclaimed Fauntleroy, and a flush overspread his
forehead. 'Will it do if I write it? I don't always spell quite
right when I haven't a dictionary and nobody tells me.'

Frances Hodgson Burnett, *Little Lord Fauntleroy* (1886)

'I don't know what you mean by "proximate".'

'Go into the surgery, and look into the dictionary then,' said he,
losing his temper for the first time during the conversation.

Elizabeth Gaskell, *Wives and Daughters* (1866)

These two novels – one written in America by Frances Hodgson
Burnett, the other by Elizabeth Gaskell in Victorian Britain –
present vivid snapshots of the identity and role of the dictionary. In
Burnett's story, seven-year-old Cedric Errol has been transplanted
from genteel poverty in New York to aristocratic splendour in
England, gaining a new identity as Lord Fauntleroy in the process.
Instructed to write a letter to his grandfather's land agent, Cedric
nevertheless lacks, as he admits, both a secure knowledge of
spelling and a dictionary. 'Is that exactly the right way to spell
"interfered"?', he asks, showing his letter to his grandfather, the
Earl of Dorincourt: 'Dear mr. Newik if you pleas mr. higins is not to
be interfeared with for the present and oblige, Yours rispecferly,

FAUNTLEROY'. As the Earl truthfully replies, '"It's not exactly the way it is spelled in the dictionary"'.

Clare Gibson, in Gaskell's *Wives and Daughters*, confesses lack of knowledge of a different kind. Her husband, a highly educated doctor, uses a polysyllabic vocabulary with ease. '"You changed your behaviour to Roger, and made him more welcome to this house than you had ever done before, regarding him as proximate heir to the Hamley estates"', he states, accusing Clare of a kind of fortune-hunting by proxy. Clare is, however, baffled. What does 'proximate' mean? As in many fictional images of marital discord, Dr and Mrs Gibson do not speak the same language. Clare is despatched to consult the dictionary in search of remedy and resolution.

Gaskell and Burnett clearly expected their own books, as works of fiction, to be read. Importantly, however, the dictionary as book already seems to stand apart. Clare Gibson is told not to read but to 'look into' the dictionary. 'That's the way with words of more than one syllable; you have to look in the dictionary', as Cedric likewise acknowledges, setting out to rewrite his letter. There are, of course, always a few stalwart individuals who choose to read entire dictionaries from cover to cover. Samuel Johnson's *Dictionary* of 1755 was, for instance, read by the Victorian poet Robert Browning as part of his self-imposed training for the art of poetry; the American writer Ammon Shea recently tackled the 20,000 pages plus of the *Oxford English Dictionary*. Like Clare or Cedric, however, ordinary dictionary-users are usually rather different. Prompted by a moment of linguistic indecision or uncertainty, or perhaps by simple curiosity about an aspect of word history or use, readers of dictionaries will usually tend to refer to or consult relatively small sections in search of particular aspects of information or advice.

Images of identity and the dictionary can, as here, neatly centre on its role as a factual work of reference by which particular aspects of

> **pe·ruse** (pə rōōz′) *vt.* --rused′, --rus′·ing [LME *perusen*, to use up, prob. < L *per-*, intens. + ME *usen*, to USE] **1** [Obs.] to examine in detail; scrutinize **2** to read carefully or thoroughly; study **3** to read in a casual or leisurely way —**pe·rus′er** *n.*

1. The anatomy of a dictionary entry: *peruse* (*Webster's New World College Dictionary*, 4th edition, Macmillan USA (1999))

language (or languages) can be checked or explored. As Figure 1 illustrates, even a relatively brief entry in a dictionary, here for the word *peruse*, will contain a striking amount of detail. Just one line provides information on its spelling, pronunciation (and expected stress pattern), as well as on part of speech and the different forms it takes in the past tense (*perused*), and the present participle (*perusing*). A further line allows us to trace word history or etymology. *Peruse*, we are told, derives from late Middle English *perusen* which had the sense 'to use up'; this itself, as a further detail adds, consists of a loan from Latin (*per*) combined with Middle English *usen*, 'to use'. Two more lines narrate the story of its use in English, presented in a carefully numbered series of senses which separate out distinct areas of meaning. The usage label 'Obs.' or 'obsolete' concisely signals the loss of the first sense ('to examine in detail; scrutinize') in modern use. The careful use of bold, italics, and typographical symbols, moreover, makes sure that the different strands of information are presented as clearly as possible. 'Helpfulness should be the ideal of a dictionary', as the American lexicographer Isaac Funk stated at the end of the 19th century. It is a maxim which still holds true.

Looking it up in the dictionary

The common idioms of English ('Look it up in the dictionary', 'What does the dictionary say?', 'Have you checked the dictionary?') can suggest a quiet certainty about the shared identity of 'the dictionary' and the information it provides. In reality, however, dictionaries are far from uniform. Size, language, and intended audience all bring diversity. Dictionaries can be monolingual, bilingual, or can exist as vast online multilingual works such as *Wiktionary* which, as its website proclaims, currently incorporates over 150 languages. They can encompass dead or living languages or both simultaneously. They can be dedicated to particular language varieties, as in the *English Dialect Dictionary* published in 1898–1905 by Joseph Wright, or the vast and still ongoing *Dictionary of American Regional English*. Style prompts still other forms of lexicographic enquiry, as in Eric Partridge's celebrated *Dictionary of Slang and Unconventional English* which contains entries such as *pollrumptious* ('unruly or restless') or the evocative *polish the king's iron with one's eyebrows* (defined as 'to be in gaol and look through the iron gated windows').

Dictionaries can also be miniature, pocket, one volume, two, or more. The second edition of the *Oxford English Dictionary* (which was published in 1989) consisted of 20 volumes and 21,730 pages; the Dutch *Woordenboek der Nederlandsche Taal*, in 43 volumes, was even bigger. Even one-volume dictionaries vary considerably. Looking a word up in Isaac Funk's single-volume *Standard Dictionary of the English Language* – which, when first published in 1893, contained 2,318 pages and weighed over five and a half kilos – was distinctly challenging. Dictionary stands – special articles of furniture on which such large unabridged dictionaries could rest – proved both popular and necessary in late 19th-century/early 20th-century America, permitting reference with less risk of injury.

Variable too, of course, are the ways in which we might now choose to look something up. If a book probably still remains the stereotypical image of 'the dictionary', a dictionary today can also be on a CD-ROM, online, on an 'app' on a mobile phone. 'Now you can get the words you want and the definitions you need while on the go!', as the Australian *Macquarie Dictionary* website promises, depicting a dictionary as a kind of virtual companion, unconstrained by weight or space. *E-dictionary* (plural *e-dictionaries*), explains the relevant entry in *Wiktionary*, is 'A dictionary in electronic form'; 'An electronic device dedicated to providing a dictionary. *Our new e-dictionary is available online or on CD-ROM*; *I put my e-dictionary in my backpack and headed off to school*', as the accompanying sample sentences state.

Rather than a single and monolithic model of 'the dictionary', modern dictionaries are therefore often better seen as commodities, precisely tailored to different audiences and different contexts of use – whether native speakers or language learners, children or adults, general reference or school text, for instance. This affects not only size, and the decisions which might have to be taken on whether or not to include particular words or senses, but also how – and in how much detail – words and meanings are to be defined. If we look up, say, *popular* in Chambers' *Junior Illustrated Dictionary* and again in *OED Online* (the third and ongoing revision of the *Oxford English Dictionary*), we will be confronted by very different results. 'Something that is popular is liked by a lot of people' states the simple definition (and single sense) given by the former. In the *OED* eight main senses (and four subsenses), each supported by a set of illustrative and dated quotations, instead reveal an extraordinary level of elaboration (see Figure 2) – precisely in line, of course, with its own identity as a scholarly dictionary on historical principles.

Defining styles, as these examples suggest, can also vary markedly between different forms of 'the dictionary'. The Chambers *Junior Illustrated Dictionary* adopts a pattern of full-sentence definition for *popular* (a style which, while earlier used in a wide range of dictionaries, now tends to characterize works aimed at children and learners). It thereby deliberately avoids the kind of elliptical style or 'dictionaryese' which instead hallmarks dictionaries aimed at adult native speakers. 'Of the people;

7.

a. Liked or admired by many people, or by a particular person or group.

1608 G. CHAPMAN *Conspiracie Duke of Byron* II. i. sig. D, He is a foole that keepes them with more care, Then they keepe him, safe, rich, and populare.

1710 *Tatler* No. 190. ¶4 This..will make me more popular among my Dependants.

1740 W. OLDYS *Life Sir Walter Ralegh* 36 Ralegh, knowing the Lord Roch to be a powerful and popular Man among the Irish, so suddenly commanded all his Company to be in Readiness by Eleven a-Clock that Night.

1795 H. H. BRACKENRIDGE *Incidents of Insurrection in Western Parts Pennsylvania* iii. 22 He has been before that time the most popular man in Allegheny county.

1812 *Religionism* 24 The popular Preachers,—men of high renown.

1884 W. BESANT *Dorothy Forster* I. xi. 288 Mr. Hilyard was popular among those who knew nothing of his scholarship and fine qualities, because he was never known to fall under the table while there was another man still sitting up.

1924 P. G. WODEHOUSE *Bill the Conqueror* 22 Breakfast was never a popular meal with those who had enjoyed overnight the hospitality of Judson Coker.

1971 *Gourmet* Feb. 58/3 About fifty years ago, when I was a child, a raisin-topped, spongelike, lemon-flavored cookie was popular.

1991 R. R. McCAMMON *Boy's Life* I. i. 8, I had a small group of friends..but I wasn't what you might call popular.

2. Part of the entry for *popular*, taken from the *OED Online*

pleasing to, enjoying the favour of or prevailing among the people', *Chambers Dictionary* – the adult counterpart of its junior text – hence states, here defining the same word in a very different way.

How much detail different readers are assumed to want – or indeed to need – when they decide to look things up is equally important in considering features such as etymology, or word origin. As the following textbox illustrates, information on etymology – here for *vaccine* – can be provided in considerable detail, tracing a line of descent through different languages and related forms. Other dictionaries can, in contrast, reveal very different processes of decision-making and design.

Etymologies of *vaccine*

> French *vaccin*, from *vaccine* cowpox, from New
> Latin *vaccina* (in *variolae vaccinae* cowpox), from
> Latin, feminine of *vaccinus*, adjective, of or from
> cows, from *vacca* cow; akin to Sanskrit *vaśa* cow.
>
> *Merriam-Webster Online English Dictionary*
>
> It is called **vaccine** from the Latin word *vacca*
> meaning 'cow' because the first vaccine was taken
> from cows.
>
> *The Oxford Primary School Dictionary*

Like many other dictionaries, *The Oxford Primary School
Dictionary* has also chosen to provide selective etymologies. Word
history is narrated where it is seen as particularly interesting or
informative, as in the entry for *petrify* ('The word **petrify** comes
from a Greek word *petra* meaning 'rock' or 'stone'. Originally it
means 'to turn something into stone'); elsewhere, the dictionary
can simply remain silent. Electronic dictionaries such as *OED
Online* place such decisions in the hands of the users themselves;
more material can be accessed for those interested in the nuances
of historical change and development.

Pronunciation offers still more options for 'the dictionary'. Should
the dictionary-maker use the International Phonetic Alphabet so
that *vaccine* is, for instance, transcribed as /'væksin/, *vaccinate* as
/'væksineit/. While more accurate, this is also more complex – and
perhaps more off-putting? – with its range of unfamiliar symbols.
Or should pronunciation be indicated by a form of respelling, with
or without additional diacritics, so that *vaccine* is represented by,
say, 'vakseen', or perhaps 'vaks-īn'? Or perhaps, as in the 2009
Collins English Dictionary, pronunciation should be omitted
altogether? Decisions on pronunciation also involve the selection
of a particular accent or accents; the decision in British

dictionaries for much of the 20th century to base information on an accent known as 'received pronunciation' served, for example, to exclude some 95% of the population. Even now, transcriptions tend to be based on southern rather than northern speech (involving different distributions of sounds and, at times, different sounds altogether).

Innovations in the use of sound files in modern electronic or digital dictionaries, moreover, mean that dictionary-users now have the opportunity not only to look things up in the dictionary – but to listen to them too. Even so, sound files will still, of course, reflect similar processes of decision-making in terms of which accent (or accents) is to be recorded. Nevertheless, they neatly circumvent the difficulties of notation – and the challenges to comprehension this can pose. The direct access to spoken forms which sound files enable can be immensely useful – especially for learners of foreign languages or those unsure about, say, the stress patterns in a given word (is it *prevaricate* or *pre'varicate*, for example?).

Even spelling, which might seem relatively unproblematic, will on closer examination reveal a number of fault-lines in 'the dictionary'. Spelling is, after all, still one of the most frequent reasons for a dictionary to be consulted. Nevertheless, for all dictionary-makers, spelling will, to some extent, involve selection from a range of variants. If one spelling is selected in a dictionary as the form for a particular headword, this does not mean that all other co-existing spellings are necessarily wrong or inadmissible. Spellings like *ageing* and *aging* instead co-exist, as do, say, *useable* and *usable, judgement* and *judgment, standardize* or *standardise*. Different dictionaries can make different decisions on the forms they prefer as headwords (and the number of variants they decide to give). On the other hand, an entirely united front is presented on spellings such as *interfear* and *rispecferly* which, in Burnett's novel, were made to challenge Cedric's knowledge of orthography and its expected forms.

Glimpses from behind the scenes of dictionary-making can be particularly illuminating here. James Murray, editor in chief of the first edition of the *Oxford English Dictionary* (the publication of which spanned 1884 to 1928) regularly received letters demanding definitive verdicts on particular forms. *Pigmy* and *pygmy* 'are about equally common', Murray replied to one such correspondent. For the dictionary, 'we slightly prefer Pygmy, tho'', as he admitted, 'we might be outvoted in a plebiscite'. *Whiskey* and *whisky* presented other areas of uncertainty. 'Both forms are current and equally correct or incorrect', Murray wrote. He suggested a stylistic compromise rather than any absolute notions of correctness: 'when in a hurry you may save a fraction of time by writing whisky, and when lingering over it you may prolong it to whiskey ... in matters of taste there is no "correct" or "incorrect"; there is the liberty of the subject.'

As Murray's letters indicate, dictionary-making can be less a matter of recording a set of definitive verdicts about language than of making a series of informed choices about the forms which, in various ways, are to be included.

Dictionary-makers must, in essence, negotiate a range of different pathways through available evidence, defining in different ways, and with reference to different selections from the vocabulary. The task of making a dictionary is rarely simple.

The dictionary as guide

'Reference books are ones that you look at when you need specific information or facts about a subject', *Collins Cobuild Dictionary* explains under *reference*: 'Reference is the act of consulting someone or something in order to get information or advice'. That dictionaries are works of fact and not fiction is an important part of their identity; it is this, for example, which underpins their widespread association with qualities such as trustworthiness and reliability, authoritativeness and truth.

Fallibilities can, of course, occasionally appear. 'Ignorance, pure ignorance', Samuel Johnson is reputed to have replied when asked how he had managed to define *pastern* as 'the knee of an horse' in the first edition of his dictionary (a corrected version – 'That part of the leg of a horse between the joint next the foot and the hoof' – appeared in later editions). In general, however, dictionaries tend to be approached as quintessentially neutral texts, ones that guide their users to an accurate understanding of words and their various ramifications, whether in terms of, say, the history of *treacle* (which in fact derives from the Greek for 'pertaining to a wild animal') or the current meanings of *random* (which, since the 1970s, has acquired the sense 'peculiar, strange, nonsensical', alongside earlier meanings of 'haphazard, lacking a definite aim or purpose').

The nature of the guidance that dictionaries provide can nevertheless reveal some interesting variations. What is presented, or indeed perceived, as a 'fact' will vary in illuminating ways. If we compare the 'same' entry over time, we can easily see the ways in which dictionaries act as witnesses to change in both culture and language, tracking the pulse of history in terms of innovation and understanding. New words, for instance, readily attest new forms within material culture, whether in past or present usage. Thomas Blount, a 17th-century lexicographer, decided, for instance, to include an explanation of an innovatory substance ('a kind of compound drink, made and so called by the Indians, the principal ingredient, is a fruit called *Cacao*, which is about the bigness of a great black fig') in his own dictionary, the *Glossographia* which was published in 1656. *Chocolate*, as thus defined by Blount, would, as later dictionaries confirm, gradually be seen not only as a drink but as something to be eaten too. 'Eaten in various comfits' especially 'a sweetmeat in the form of bars, cakes, and drops', stated the first edition of the *OED*. An entry written in 1889, this in turn evokes its own image of obsolescence. *Sweetmeat* is 'archaic', modern dictionaries record. '**Chocolate** is a sweet hard food made from cocoa beans. It is usually brown in colour and is eaten as a sweet', the most recent edition of *Collins Cobuild Dictionary* instead declares.

As here, the passage of time changes the narratives that dictionaries tell, both in terms of words themselves, and in the meanings they both lose and gain. The American lexicographer Noah Webster's definition of *racoon* (a 'palatable food') in his celebrated *American Dictionary of the English Language* in 1828 is not one shared in modern dictionaries. Samuel Johnson's bleak definition of *cancer* in 1755 ('A virulent swelling, or sore, not to be cured') is also distinct from the phrasing and entries open to dictionary-makers in the 21st century. Headwords unknown to Johnson (*radiotherapy*, *chemotherapy*, *chemo*) instead trace the facts of continuing innovation and response. If we turn our gaze to more recent history, war, economic concerns, and global warming have brought forms such as *friendly fire*, *credit crunch*, or *quantitative easing* as well as *carbon footprint* and *carbon offset*, or *ecoterrorism* and *ecocatastrophe* which also variously find their way into dictionaries and the ongoing story of language and language use. *Big Society* was declared the 'word of the year' by Oxford dictionaries in November 2010.

If the facts that dictionaries record are themselves open to change, so too are the attitudes and opinions which dictionary definitions often reveal. Dictionaries can, for example, also act as illuminating cultural artefacts in their own right. Is *modesty*, as in Noah Webster's *American Dictionary* of 1828, really 'the richest gem in the diadem of [female] honor' and 'the sweetest charm of female excellence'? Or is it, as Webster's modern counterparts state, a quality evident in unassuming or modest behaviour, as well as in decorum and decency? Likewise, is the use of *bloody* as an intensifier empirically restricted to the 'lowest classes', as the first edition of the *OED* suggested? Or was this a 'fact' which depended more on the prevalence of particular class-based stereotypes rather than on evidence which derived from the real facts of usage?

While dictionaries are indeed reference books, information can also be filtered through particular ideological assumptions, here in relation to ideas about gender and class (though, as later chapters in this book explore, a range of social and cultural assumptions can intervene in the kind of guidance that dictionaries, at various points, might choose to offer). Behind the image of the reference book is, of course, the human – sometimes all too human – lexicographer, drawing the line on whether particular words should be included, and crafting how individual definitions are to be phrased (or particular cultural undercurrents expressed).

The dictionary as judge

Dictionary: 'A malevolent literary device for cramping the growth of a language and making it hard and inelastic', the American writer Ambrose Bierce stated in his markedly subversive *The Devil's Dictionary* of 1911. Bierce's work offers, of course, further confirmation of the mutability – and diversity – of 'the dictionary'. This particular entry, however, also focuses attention on another prevailing image of the identity of the dictionary – as a work which should provide an authorized version of language and language use, and by which ordinary usage can be corrected and controlled.

Sir, My trusty fifth edition Concise Oxford English Dictionary, which has been at my side for some 40 years since student days, fell apart recently and I was forced to buy myself a new version. My initial pleasure at having a smart new up-to-date book was rapidly tempered, however, by the discovery that the modern compilers seem to have taken on a purely descriptive role rather than a prescriptive one.

They thus endorse a number of incorrect uses such as 'comprised of' rather than 'comprise' on the ground that they have become common usage. Whereas I recognise that language has to be allowed to change in response to new requirements, it surely

> should not be allowed to change just because ignorance of the language has become widespread.
>
> I have always looked to my dictionary to serve as a guide to correct language use. That is why I have it. If it fails to perform this function, then it ceases to serve any purpose and I have wasted my money.

The letter above, sent to *The Times* in 2007, concisely illustrates the conflicts that can surround 'the dictionary' in this context. Should the good dictionary-maker describe language, recording the facts of usage according to the evidence at his or her disposal? Or is the proper role of the dictionary-maker to prescribe – to make firm recommendations about what should, or should not, be used? What, moreover, is the nature of correctness? And how is the lexicographer to decide?

At stake in this particular letter is a change in progress within English usage. If older writers and speakers tended to use constructions such as 'the book comprises six chapters', recent usage instead reveals the currency of an alternative construction – 'the book is comprised of six chapters'. Both constructions therefore now exist in the facts of usage – and in the descriptive authority of the language itself. It is *descriptive authority* of this kind which likewise tends to inform the working of modern lexicography. Entries are based on careful analysis of evidence, providing authoritative – and objective – information on the realities of language in use. In the disputed entry for *comprise*, authority of this kind has clearly informed the changes that have been made in the newly revised edition – information is brought up to date in a process which is, of course, entirely in keeping with the expected accuracy of the dictionary as reference book.

From a linguistic point of view, change itself is entirely neutral. Living languages are constantly on the move, changing the ways in which words are used, as well as the structures and meanings open to their users. Popular attitudes to change can, however – as the letter also indicates – be rather different. As in the charges of 'incorrectness' and 'ignorance', it can be tempting to see new forms as evidence of decline and decay, of a failure to use language 'properly'. It can be equally tempting to see the identity of the dictionary as something that should, in some way, tether or anchor language. In prescriptive models of this kind, the role of the dictionary-maker moves towards that of judge and perhaps censor, providing verdicts on the legitimacy or otherwise of particular forms. Change, by extension, is to be resisted.

The images of *prescriptive authority* that result can be distinctly authoritarian. As in a number of earlier dictionaries, evidence on the facts of current usage can be deliberately set aside. Instead, the weight of opinion, or the pull of language attitudes, is made to inform lexicographical judgement on which usages are to be found wanting (and correspondingly condemned) – or which are to be preferred. We can see a similar process at work, for instance, in Samuel Johnson's highly prescriptive entry for the word *shabby* in his dictionary of 1755.

> SHABBY. *adj.* [A word that has crept into conversation and low writing; but ought not to be admitted into the language.]
> Mean; paltry.

As in the conflicted response to *comprise/comprise of*, the full entry for *shabby* neatly illustrates the conflict between *norms of usage* (the facts of language in use) and what we can instead see as *language attitudes*, a rather more nebulous territory in which convictions or beliefs about what 'should' be used can instead come into play. *Shabby* was, for instance, widely in use in the descriptive realities of 18th-century English. Quotations supplied by Johnson (e.g. 'the dean was so shabby', as used by the writer Jonathan Swift) act as witnesses to language practice, here within the written language of books (though we can assume the existence of corresponding patterns in spoken language too). Descriptive evidence is nevertheless countered by prescriptive opinion and overtly proscriptive judgement. *Shabby* 'ought not to be admitted into the language', Johnson declares. Like *comprise of*, even if it is used, it shouldn't be. Authority here intentionally reaches beyond the dictionary, changing the course of language in use.

Disconcertingly – and not least for the status of the dictionary as reference book – popular images of prescriptive authority can, as here, also critically depend upon the decision to ignore or disregard the facts of usage, and their implications. Such tensions about the role and identity of dictionaries are, as we will see at various points in this book, widely prevalent in the history of dictionary-making. Change, and how it is to be recorded, is a pervasive source of conflict in the relationship between dictionaries and language as well as between dictionaries and their users. Taking the long view of language and lexicography can nevertheless be useful. *Shabby* – entirely irrespective of Johnson's censure – would, of course, continue in use, hence presenting its own authority for the history of the language, and the words and meanings which exist within it. Language here clearly has the upper hand. The same is true of *comprise* and *comprise of*, in spite of the protestations which might be evident in contemporary language attitudes. Images of control – narratives in which the language should obey the lexicographer – though pervasive, are, as we will see in Chapter 4, also habitually illusory.

While dictionaries must provide information on 'correct' rather than 'incorrect' forms, it is in descriptive rather than prescriptive correctness that the evidence in modern dictionaries therefore determinedly resides. In this context, as publishing history alone reminds us, the dictionary is a highly mutable text, bound to change and not stasis. In a living language, new and revised editions of dictionaries continually narrate the changing history of the words we use, and the ways we come to use them. As Ephraim Chambers, another famous 18th-century lexicographer, stressed, the lexicographer is necessarily like the historian, bound to follow behind the facts, gathering and assembling them – rather than creating them in advance.

The labyrinth of words

Dictionaries, in spite of their familiarity, can therefore be framed in countless fictions (the dictionary as arbiter or judge, the dictionary as control, the dictionary as a record of 'good' words, or words fit to live). Such mistaken identities are pervasive. In reality, of course, dictionaries instead reveal a wide-ranging engagement with words, meanings, artefacts, usage, and culture – and, as we will see, the perspectives which might variously be taken on different cultures and different words. Popularly seen in terms of constraint and regulation, and as defending rather than describing the language, dictionaries instead profoundly engage with how we, as speakers, understand the world and articulate the nature of what we perceive – documenting too the changes which have taken place within such perceptions, or in the varying idioms and expressions which we may come to use.

They also, and more fundamentally, reveal the ways in which language, characterized by its superabundance of words and meanings ('the boundless chaos of a living speech', as Johnson described it; a 'labyrinth', as Blount had earlier and evocatively noted in his *Glossographia*), can be presented in an ordered way, one which genuinely does facilitate reference and enquiry. Regulation in this sense is vital if the dictionary is to serve its true purpose in enabling reference to be made to its entries. As the title page of the Swiss-born Guy Miège's *Great French Dictionary* of 1688 proclaimed, a dictionary, in a variety of ways, promises us language 'orderly digested' – a text in which words and senses are divided, their various characteristics analysed, and set down in a carefully determined structure.

A

Table Alphabeticall, con-
teyning and teaching the true
vvriting, and vnderstanding of hard
vsuall English wordes, borrowed from
the Hebrew, Greeke, Latine,
or French. &c.

With the interpretation thereof by
plaine English words, gathered for the benefit &
helpe of Ladies, Gentlewomen, or any other
vnskilfull persons.

Whereby they may the more easilie
and better vnderstand many hard English
wordes, vvhich they shall heare or read in
Scriptures, Sermons, or elswhere, and also
be made able to vse the same aptly
themselues.

Legere, et non intelligere , neglegere est.
As good not read, as not to vnderstand.

AT LONDON,
Printed by I. R. for Edmund Wea-
uer, & are to be sold at his shop at the great
North doore of Paules Church.
1 6 0 4.

3. The title page of Robert Cawdrey's *Table Alphabeticall* (1604)

The chosen method of arrangement or the imposition of order may vary. Dictionaries are not necessarily alphabetical, but may be topical, thematic, etymological, or even phonetic in their chosen divisions; languages that do not use an alphabet, such as Japanese, can order information under the number of strokes required to create the character in question. Contents too may incline to the encyclopaedic or strictly lexical (as we will see, the divide between dictionaries and encyclopaedias remains fuzzy for much of their history). Illustration too, whether in the form of pictures or examples, may be present or absent. The essentials of identity nevertheless in this respect remain clear. As Robert Cawdrey stated in the very first monolingual dictionary of English – the *Table Alphabeticall* of 1604 – the dictionary is fundamentally a text of 'benefit & helpe' which seeks to facilitate 'better vnderstanding' as well as to aid subsequent language use. A variety of other facts (and factors) may of course intervene in these aims, and the ways in which they are realized. These, though, form important themes which will be explored in subsequent chapters of this book.

Chapter 2
History

'We must consider how very little history there is; I mean real authentick history.'

Samuel Johnson, one of the most quoted – and quotable – of lexicographers, could, as here, display certain reservations about the nature of history and historical understanding. Of course, as Johnson admitted, 'that certain Kings reigned, and certain battles were fought, we can depend upon as true'. Nevertheless, he remained resistant to its wider meanings: 'all the colouring, all the philosophy of history, is conjecture'.

History is not, however, easily disregarded in a study of lexicography. This too has its battles and its moments of rebellion. National (and international) contest can, at times, be all too visible, while images of the proper borders to be observed – and territories to be defended – have their own relevance in this respect. The 'authentick history' of dictionaries nevertheless rarely involves kings (or queens). Instead, dictionary-making is a task that has traditionally been undertaken by a wide range of ordinary individuals – clerks and teachers, governesses and clerics, monks and lawyers, scholars and writers – united by a desire to probe the nature of words and meaning and to track, as Johnson noted in his *Dictionary* of 1755, how people 'have hitherto expressed their thoughts'.

Beginnings

From a global perspective, the history of dictionaries spans
thousands of years. The earliest dictionaries – wordlists and
meanings etched into clay tablets – can be traced to Sumeria (now
part of Iraq) in c. 2000 BC. Over 30,000 still survive. A wide range
of early civilizations shared this impulse to document and
categorize language. In China, the *Erya* (variously translated as
'The Literary Expositor', 'Luxuriant and Refined Words', or
'Progress Towards Correctness') is, for example, dated to the 3rd
century BC. Arranged thematically by topic, it provides glosses or
explanations for difficult words in individual texts, as well as a wide
range of encyclopaedic information. Aristophanes of Byzantium
(c. 257–c. 180 BC), a director of the library at Alexandria, made the
first known attempt to compile a comprehensive dictionary of
Greek – the *Lexeis* or 'readings' (from *lexis* 'word' < *legein* 'to say'),
of which only fragments now survive. Even earlier, scholars in
Greece had compiled glossaries explaining the difficult words in
writers such as Homer. The range of these early works – each
carefully written by hand – is striking. Xu Shen, a Confucian
scholar and philologist, already included some 10,000 detailed
entries in his *Shuowen Jiezi* ('Discussions of Writings and
Explanations of Characters') which was written towards the end
of the 1st century AD.

Like the work of Aristophanes, many of these early texts would,
however, also prove victims of history itself. No copy survives, for
example, of the large Latin dictionary *De Significatu Verborum*
('On the Meaning of Words') compiled by the Roman grammarian
Marcus Verrius Flaccus in 20 BC. The 20-volume text (with the
same title) by Sexius Festus, which was based on this, suffered a
similar fate. Only one (damaged) manuscript survives, together
with a summary made in the 8th century.

Medieval wordhoards

Scribes and scribal culture were central to the emergence of lexicography. Long before printing, scribal culture engaged with the various ways in which the knowledge of words might be organized and transmitted. The *Etymologicae* of Isidore of Seville (c. 560–636), for example, sets out what was intended to be a compendium of knowledge, a way of understanding how words might illuminate a culture and its history – written in 20 volumes and encompassing 448 chapters. Medieval Latin dictionaries were regularly copied out by hand, testimony to the dedication of these early copyists (as well as further indicating the importance placed on texts of this kind). The late 12th-century *Derivationes* by Hugutio of Pisa still exists in around 200 manuscripts, as does John of Genoa's immense *Catholicum* of 1286 (the latter would be one of the first books to emerge in print, in 1460).

Contemporary interest in words and meaning is evident not only in self-standing works such as those mentioned above. Far more pervasive are glosses – hand-written explanations of difficult or unfamiliar words which appear between the lines (in what are known as *intralinear glosses*) or in the margins (*marginal glosses*) of individual texts. These offer an important form of proto-lexicography – a way of interpreting elements which might otherwise impede a reader's understanding as they read a particular work. Confirming an early and flourishing multilingualism, glosses in English texts often provided native equivalents for learned Latin words (*inscriptio* could, for instance, be explained by the native *inwriting*); conversely, they could simply gloss Latin into Latin, replacing harder forms by easier ones. Different readers, moreover, added different glosses, creating, in effect, a multi-layered text of interpretation (and re-interpretation) in which meaning and understanding are of profound importance.

Already present is the core two-part structure of what would later be formalized as the dictionary entry. In both, a particular item of vocabulary is paired with a corresponding definition or explanation, either within the same language or in a different one. Text-internal glosses are nevertheless much more restrictive than their later counterparts. Limited to the immediate reading experience of the text, the order in which glosses or explanations could be consulted was dictated by where they occurred in the manuscript itself. Explanation was also cut short; the space in margins – and especially that between lines – is limited. If we can see interesting affinities with our modern dictionaries, the differences are also very clear.

The glosses for an individual text could, however, also be collected up into a free-standing work (giving what is known as a *glossae collectae*). Still more significant, as in the 10th-century *Glossary* by the Anglo-Saxon monk and scholar Aelfric, is the decision to craft words and accompanying interpretations into an independent work. Aelfric's *Glossary* (of which 12 manuscripts still survive) was intended to be used in teaching Latin to Benedictine novices at Cerne Abbey in Dorset. Based on Isidore of Seville's *Etymologicae* (though deliberately much shorter), it contained a basic vocabulary of some 1,300 Latin headwords paired with Old English explanations, organized thematically rather than alphabetically under topics like wild animals or parts of the body (or, in the final section, human vices).

Aelfric, fully conversant with earlier work in Spain and within classical scholarship, also provides a swift corrective to assumptions about the insularity (or elementary nature) of medieval culture. These multilingual contexts are in fact vital for an understanding of much early lexicography, not least since monolingual vernacular lexicography was to be a far later development. John of Garland, author of another thematically organized text for teaching Latin to learners – the early 13th-century *Dictionarius* (literally, 'a collection of *dictions*' or sayings) – provides a particularly useful example of the kind of linguistic confidence that could characterize lexicography at this time. Born in England and educated at Oxford, Garland lived in France for much of his life ('Garland' in fact refers to the Clos de Garlande on the Left Bank in Paris where he lived and taught in the 1220s). He wrote the *Dictionarius* in Latin, providing interlinear glosses in French and English.

It was Latin, as the international language of scholarship, which nevertheless united lexicographical work across medieval Europe. In 11th-century Italy, Papius wrote the *Elementarium* (an alphabetically organized dictionary widely used in England for learning Latin); in France, Firmin le Ver completed his extensive Latin–French dictionary, containing over 45,000 entries, in 1440. In Spain, Alfonso de Palencia's *Universel Vocabulario en latin y en romance* appeared in 1490. Latin likewise pervaded early English lexicography, not just in the work of Aelfric and Garland, but in texts such as the eloquently named *Promptorium Parvolorum sive Clericum* (the 'storehouse for children and clerics'), the first English–Latin dictionary, which was compiled in Norfolk by a Dominican recluse called Galfridus Grammaticus in 1440.

Dictionary-making in the early modern period

The *Promptorium Parvolorum* already seems much closer to our modern sense of 'dictionary'. Garland's *Dictionarius*, for example, was a largely discursive text which, using the device of a walk through Paris, provided explanations for the various items encountered along the way. The *Promptorium* instead included over 10,000 alphabetically organized entries in which English headwords were paired with Latin equivalents, as well as brief vernacular explanations. *Fyrst* (first) is explained as 'be-forn' and is then followed by the Latin *primo*; *lyvely* is glossed as 'quik and ful of lyfe' and followed by *vivaciter*. If we move forward in time by almost a century, however, the Latin–English *Dictionary* published in 1538 by the diplomat and humanist scholar Sir

Thomas Elyot is clearly closer still. This was researched using books from the royal library of Henry VIII (to whom it is dedicated). Here explanations are often strikingly detailed and precise, as in Elyot's entry for the erudite *logodaedalus*: 'he that speaketh craftily to deceiue; or in eloquente words induceth sentences vayne, or of lyttel purpose'.

Dictionaries were well established as educational texts by this date. Latin dominated here too. John Withals, author of the *Shorte Dictionarie for Yonge Beginners*, the first edition of which appeared in 1556, specifically defines his work as 'a thynge written ... to induce chyldren to the latine tonge'. A particularly good example of the interleaved concerns of both dictionary-making and education is, however, presented by the work of John Baret, a tutor in 16th-century Cambridge. Set daily translation exercises from English into Latin, Baret's students had, he noted, simply tended to resort to Baret himself for every word they did not know. His solution had instead been to get them to craft a collective book of reference so that, each day, they recorded both English words and Latin equivalents, organized under appropriate headings. If this was originally 'wrought onely for our owne priuate vse', as Baret notes, he swiftly realized the utility of the resulting work, deciding to 'put it in print for the common profit of others, and the publike propagation of the Latin tongue'. By 1574, when the first edition of what he termed his *Alvearie* was printed, it had become a 'triple dictionary', encompassing Latin, English, and French. Six years later, as the title page announced, it was now 'quadruple', having added Greek in the interests of 'common profit' of a still more extensive kind.

Even if early modern dictionaries were now in print rather than manuscript, this didn't necessarily preclude individual readers deciding, like the scribal readers of medieval times, to add extra words or further elements of interpretation. Baret's *Alvearie*, as the image of the title page illustrates, is depicted as a metaphorical hive of industry. Here, as Baret stressed, students and readers

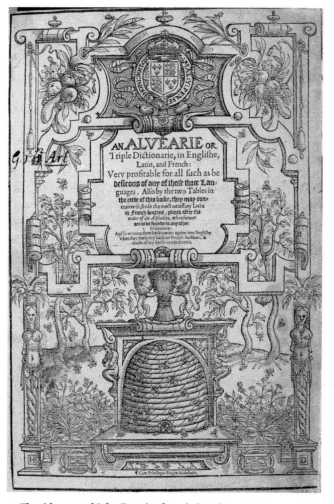

4. The title page of John Baret's *Alvearie* (1574)

could 'like diligent Bees' continue to add material 'under their proper Tytles' [i.e. the headings of the dictionary], as well as in 'the margent of this boke'. While this image of collective industry is one to which we shall return, equally important, however, is the emphasis placed by Baret (and others) on dictionaries as books to be actively used – as well as ones which, in various ways, might serve to democratize 'profyt' and knowledge throughout the nation.

Words – and the knowledge of how to use them – were, as the historian and lexicographer James Howell later argued, a fertile source of power. '*Words* are the life of Knowledge, they sett Free// And bring forth Truth by way of Midwifry', Howell declared in his polyglot *Lexicon Tetraglotton* published in 1660. As he added, it was language which served to discriminate between the gentleman and the clown, the philosopher and the fool:

> For *words* in Man bear the most Critick part,
> We speak by Nature, but speak *well* by Art;
> And as good Bells we judge of by the sound,
> So discreet Men by *words* well-plac'd are found.

Dictionaries, seen in this light, were, as Howell also contended, strikingly valuable acquisitions.

Howell's work (which encompassed English, French, Italian, and Spanish) also confirms the growing role of dictionaries at this time as interpreters between different vernacular languages (rather than merely between classical and vernacular languages). This was a further important development in Renaissance lexicography. The first French–English dictionary – John Palsgrave's *Lesclarcissement de la langue francoyse* – in fact dates from 1530. Like Baret, Palsgrave early saw the utility of practical lexicography – of texts that could be used not just in decoding foreign languages but which might aid in their active use. Education again provided the spur. While the material which Palsgrave included in the dictionary drew on his earlier experience as French tutor to Henry VIII's sister Mary (who married Louis XII of France in 1514), such knowledge would, in the form of a dictionary, now serve a far wider purpose: 'by mean of my poore labours taken on this occasion/ the French tongue may herafter by others the more easely be taught/ & also be attained … by suche/ as … shalbe desyrous'.

The sheer range of bilingual works in early modern lexicography – in which English is variously paired with French, Spanish, Dutch, Italian, Greek, Welsh, Portuguese, or Amerindian (as well, of course, as Latin) – can, in fact, sit uncomfortably against modern stereotypes in which English speakers are usually deemed to possess marked incapacity in acquiring other languages. Similar multilingualism is evident across Europe: dictionaries of French and Flemish appear in 1552, French and Spanish in 1562, and French and English in 1570.

If education, as we have seen, provided one domain in which Renaissance lexicography flourished, commerce (and contact through trade and exploration) offered another. Renaissance history is, of course, also distinguished by the marked widening of geographical as well as intellectual horizons. Trade and trading hence presented a wide range of multilingual contexts in which dictionaries might prove themselves of value (merchants, for example, often make their appearance among the kinds of readers overtly specified by contemporary dictionary-makers on their title pages as well as in their prefatory matter). Early lexicographers, as this also indicates, were by no means unaware of the commercial potential of their own work. Dictionaries could, in turn, acquire a strikingly ambitious scope and range, even if, in doing so, they could at times also assume identities unforeseen by their original compilers. The Dutch writer Noel de Berlaimont's *Vocabulare* – which began life in a now lost bilingual first edition of 1530 – would, for instance, become a topically organized work in four languages (French, Flemish, Latin, and Spanish) by 1551, and six languages by 1576 (when English and German were added). By 1639, it existed as a 'little Dictionary of Eight

Languages' (specified as Latin, French, Low-Dutch, High-Dutch, Spanish, Italian, English, and 'Portvgall'). It too proclaimed itself as 'perfected and made fit for TRAVELLERS, young MERCHANTS and SEA-MEN, especially those that desire to attaine to the use of these Tongues'.

In a further innovation at this time, double or bidirectional dictionaries also make their appearance, further increasing the intended utility of lexicography and enabling readers – whether merchants or otherwise – to choose either language as source or target language. John Rider (a tutor in Oxford who would later become a bishop in Ireland) hence persuasively urged the ways in which his *Bibliotecha Scholastica* – a 'double dictionary' of English/Latin and Latin/English produced in 1589 – was 'very profitable and necessarie' for 'factors or marchants' as well as 'courtiers' and 'clarkes', 'scholars' and 'apprentices'. Latin, as Rider suggests, was not merely a language of scholarship but a practical lingua franca, enabling communication between nations in a range of contexts.

The rise of native monolingual dictionaries

Until the very end of the 16th century, contemporary images of 'the dictionary' were dominated by the classical languages, and by bilingual or multilingual works. That a dictionary might devote itself solely to a modern vernacular language such as French or Italian, documenting native words and meanings in their own right, was without precedent. The work of language academies such as the Accademia della Crusca (established in Italy in 1582) was nevertheless to embody an important reorientation in lexicography. Swiftly declaring its intention to craft a normative dictionary of Italian, the Accademia sought to affirm both the status and significance of the native tongue. As its chosen name ('the academy of the bran') suggests, its remit was strongly interventionist. By means of its dictionary, the 'chaff' of language was to be discarded. Only that judged of value would be retained and represented.

Other nations followed suit; the French, Italians, and Spanish were already at work 'expounding their own words by their own language', wrote Richard Mulcaster, a gifted schoolmaster and scholar, in his *Elementarie* which was published in London in 1582. The scale of such vernacular lexicography could be impressive. Jean Nicot's extensive *Thresor de la langue françoyse* was published in 1606, containing 18,000 entries which detailed both older and more modern forms. Likewise in Spain, Sebastian de Covarrubias, the chaplain to the king, crafted the detailed *Tesoro de la lengua castellana o española* (1611), as well as a lengthy supplement in manuscript. The projected *Vocabolario* of the Accademia della Crusca appeared in the following year, spanning 1,000 pages. A further edition followed in 1624.

For Mulcaster, as he noted with regret, monolingual English lexicography already seemed to lag behind. Even if the English were 'skilfull' abroad, they were, he argued, 'ignorant at home'. No 'English Academy' existed to reform speech by means of a dictionary of the native tongue. Mulcaster's *Elementarie* instead established what was, in effect, to be the first proposal for a monolingual English dictionary. Here he set out a 'generall table' – a list of 8,000 words including loanwords such as *ceremony* or *certification*, *desecrate* and *desolate*, as well as native forms such as *dark* and *dank* – which such a work should include in order to enable the English to 'know what we both write and speak'. Mulcaster's lexicographic ambitions drew in other ways too on the normative impulses of language academies abroad; such a dictionary, as Mulcaster added, should aim to expound not only the 'naturall sense' of words but also their 'proper vse'.

Over 20 years, however, would elapse before the first English monolingual dictionary was published – the slight *Table Alphabeticall* written by Robert Cawdrey, a Rutland schoolmaster, in 1604. This was a work very different in scope and scale to those being produced on the Continent. Containing some 2,500 words in 117 pages, the *Table* deliberately engaged with a narrow subset of the vocabulary, focusing on what Cawdrey described as 'hard vsuall English wordes' – loanwords such as the Latin-derived *congratulate* (explained as 'to reioyce with another for some good fortune') or the French-derived *consent* (which he glossed as 'agreement').

Mulcaster had earlier emphasized the problems caused by the 'great traffik' of new and foreign words within Renaissance writing; Cawdrey's text – like a number of subsequent English dictionaries – would therefore aim to remove some of the disempowerment which ordinary speakers could feel when faced by difficult, unfamiliar, and 'hard' words – especially those deriving from the learned terrains of Latin and Greek. Addressed to *Ladies, Gentlewomen, or any other vnskilfull persons*, other entries in his dictionary, for instance, explained classical loanwords such as *exorbitant* ('out of order, measure, or place') or new Latin loans such as *nuncupatory*, defined as 'telling or declaring any thing' (and for which our earliest evidence still dates from 1603).

Cawdrey's *Table* also usefully illustrates other crosscurrents in contemporary lexicography. While dictionaries have so far perhaps been depicted as entirely independent works, it is clear that dictionary-making was, in reality, often instead an exercise in careful and, at times, creative appropriation. Cawdrey, for example, depended heavily on the *English Schoole-maister*, a work published by the Cambridge-educated Edmund Coote in 1596. Not a dictionary, this nevertheless also contained a 'table' of 1,700 words for which brief explanations were provided. *Unsatiable*, for instance, was accompanied by the definition 'that hath not enogh'; *transfigure* was explained by 'change'.

If this is perhaps the real beginning of monolingual English lexicography, Coote's work (and its own patterns of assimilation and addition through time) also affirms the kind of accretive, cumulative structuring that is also important in the history of dictionaries (and which was, as we have seen, early evident in Aelfric's considered use of Isidore of Seville). If Cawdrey appropriates Coote, he also adds and changes, as well as incorporating words from his own reading of other works, including other dictionaries in Latin.

Contemporary dictionaries can, as a result, appear less as self-standing, independent works than ones which depend on a web of influences and intertextuality. Judicious use of what has gone before can, as we will see in Chapter 3, inform considered innovation and change, addition and revision. Injudicious appropriation can, on the other hand, once again remind us that lexicography is not always the neutral activity we might initially assume. Blount's *Glossographia*, for instance, which itself combines the results of independent reading with a careful scrutiny of other dictionaries in French, Italian, Latin, and English, was appropriated by John Milton's nephew, Edward Phillips, in 1658 in a dictionary entitled *New World of Words*. While such words may have been new to Phillips, they certainly weren't to Blount. 'Must this be suffred?', Blount expostulated in *A World of Errors Discovered in the New World of Words*, censuring Phillips as a 'lexicographical mercenary' who had published 'the fruit of above twenty years spare hours' as his own. Judicious lexicographers should of course also give credit where credit is due. Blount, unlike Phillips, scrupulously acknowledges his own sources, and his debts to them.

Dictionaries in the 18th century

The 'hard word' tradition which we can see at work in Cawdrey's *Table Alphabeticall* (or equally in, say, John Bullokar's *English Expositor* which, published in 1616, was directed, as its title page explains, to *Teaching the Interpretation of the Hardest Words used in our Language*) could establish a particularly enduring image of 'the dictionary', and what it should contain. Samuel Johnson's 1755 dictionary, for example, still includes entries for such 'hard' words as *tripudiary* ('performed by dancing') and *anatiferous* ('producing ducks'). Its language is often formal, avoiding what he described as 'colloquial barbarity'. The sense that dictionaries might also be more comprehensive (and thereby also more widely useful), however, also gradually emerges. John Kersey's *New English Dictionary* of 1702, for example, deliberately countered expectations that it would contain a 'monstrous Heap of difficult and abstruse Terms'. Instead, as Kersey stressed, a dictionary could be a 'compleat collection' of the 'Most Proper and Significant Words, commonly used in the Language'.

Dictionary-making during this century, in fact, reveals a range of competing trends. The continuing popularity of encyclopaedic dictionaries was clear, as in Nathaniel Bailey's *Universal Etymological English Dictionary* published in 1721, or in the continued success in France of Richelet's celebrated *Dictionnaire françois, contenant les mots et les choses*, first published in 1680. Bailey's, like a number of 18th-century dictionaries, included information on local towns – and even local market days. Conversely, Samuel Johnson contended that dictionaries should omit features such as proper names and geographical information in order to focus on the vocabulary alone. While Johnson defended the inclusion of 'easy' words such as *dog* or *mouse* (the latter memorably defined as 'The smallest of all beasts; a little animal haunting houses and corn fields, destroyed by cats'), other writers nevertheless argued against the self-evident folly of including words that everyone knew anyway. 'This Dictionary will be found better calculated ... than any hitherto extant; as it is not crowded with the common Words of the language, such as every person must be supposed to understand', as the printer John Baskerville declared in his compact *Vocabulary, or Pocket Dictionary* which appeared in 1765.

The image of prescriptive authority which was popularly embedded in language academies, and the dictionaries they produced, also remained powerful. The first edition of the dictionary of the Académie Française (founded in 1635) had appeared in 1694, the second in 1718, the third in 1740. Spain founded its own language academy – the Real Academia Española – in 1713, producing the six-volume *Diccionario de la lengua castellana* in 1726–39. That a dictionary might, in itself, control language was an ideal that academies across Europe served to foster, bringing to the fore issues such as correctness and purity, regulation and restraint. Normative dictionaries of this kind often sought to delimit usage, issuing edicts on good and bad usage, of acceptable and unacceptable words and meanings.

Here too, however, as Chapter 4 will further explore, dissent and division could be marked. Samuel Johnson's original 'idea of an English dictionary' in 1747 was, for example, closely aligned with ideals outlined for French by the Académie Française; English would, Johnson argued, be both fixed and purified by his work, while the proposed remit of the lexicographer was distinctly authoritarian, offering prescriptive 'jurisdiction' as well as a remedy for the flux of speech. Eight years later, the position articulated in the preface to the finished dictionary was nevertheless very different:

> Academies have been instituted, to guard the avenues of their language, to retain fugitives, and repulse intruders; but their vigilance and activity have hitherto been vain; … to enchain syllables, and to lash the wind, are equally the undertakings of pride, unwilling to measure its desires by its strength.

Authority, as Johnson realized, was productive of its own conflicts; the fact that the French Academy had felt it necessary to issue successive editions of its dictionary clearly suggested that language was not so easily reduced to rule. An uneasy distance lay between the rhetoric of prescription (and proscription) and the kind of evidence that language in use continued to present. The shackles by which the dictionary-maker might seek to enchain syllables were, it seems, often cast aside in the realities of a living speech.

5. Samuel Johnson and the illusion of control

History and the historical method

It was history itself which provided the impetus for a number of
new directions in 19th-century dictionary-making. While language
academies had, as we have seen, tended to stress the need for
dictionary-makers to intervene in language usage, Franz Passow, a
German scholar and classical lexicographer, instead emphasized
the ways in which the study of language through time could, in
effect, create a new form of lexicographical narrative.
Chronologically ordered quotations featuring the word in
question, he argued, instead offered the potential for words to 'tell
their own story'. In turn, the role of the lexicographer should
simply be to recount the facts, the empirically garnered evidence of
change. Evidence rather than opinion (or authoritarian edict) was
in turn seen as forming the proper basis for definition, and for
exploring how words were really used.

The historical method which Passow's *Handwörterbuch der
griechischen Sprache* (1819–23) embodied was to be highly

influential. Philology in the 19th century presented a radical rethinking of what dictionaries might be said to do. The emphasis on the sovereignty of the raw material – on lexicography as a disciplined and descriptive engagement with facts, verified through the construction of an extensive and accurate collection of quotations (and analysed without the intrusion of personal likes or dislikes) – would fundamentally change the course of lexicography. In what is often described as a philological revolution, descriptivism – the duty of the dictionary-maker to describe language as it is – here displaced the fallibilities of attempted prescriptive rule.

Across Europe, vast scholarly dictionaries took shape. Jacob and Wilhelm Grimm began work in 1838 on a historical dictionary of German – the celebrated *Deutsches Wörterbuch* – which finally reached completion, with over 350,000 entries, in 1960. Evidence was gathered through a spirit of national enterprise; volunteers across the nation were asked to read books and send in precisely dated quotations. Émile Littré similarly adopted the historical method in his *Dictionnaire de la langue française* (often known as 'Le Littré'), a work which, completed in 1873, had taken almost 30 years of scrupulous research. In Holland, Matthias de Vries began work on the *Woordenboek der Nederlansche Taal*, publication of which spanned 1864 to 1998 (work on it began in 1850).

The *OED* (or, as its original title stated, *A New English Dictionary on Historical Principles*) was likewise a collaborative venture on this model. Across the globe, 'English-speaking and English-reading' people' had been involved in gathering the vital evidence on which the dictionary was built. The scale of this work – especially in an era before computers – is daunting. Over six million 'slips', each with a dated and attributed quotation, were sent in for the first edition. Over 25 years of research preceded publication of its first part in 1884 (which merely covered the words in *A–Ant*). Another 44 years would be required before its final part appeared.

AN APPEAL

TO THE

ENGLISH-SPEAKING AND ENGLISH-READING PUBLIC

TO READ BOOKS AND MAKE EXTRACTS FOR

THE PHILOLOGICAL SOCIETY'S

NEW ENGLISH DICTIONARY.

IN November 1857, a paper was read before the Philological Society by Archbishop Trench, then Dean of Westminster, on 'Some Deficiencies in our English Dictionaries,' which led to a resolution on the part of the Society to prepare a Supplement to the existing Dictionaries supplying these deficiencies. A very little work on this basis sufficed to show that to do anything effectual, not a mere Dictionary-Supplement, but a new Dictionary worthy of the English Language and of the present state of Philological Science, was the object to be aimed at. Accordingly, in January 1859, the Society issued their 'Proposal for the publication of a New English Dictionary,' in which the characteristics of the proposed work were explained, and an appeal made to the English and American public to assist in collecting the raw materials for the work, these materials consisting of quotations illustrating the use of English words by all writers of all ages and in all senses, each quotation being made on a uniform plan on a half-sheet of notepaper, that they might in due course be arranged and classified alphabetically and significantly. This Appeal met with a generous response: some hundreds of volunteers began to read books, make quotations, and send in their slips to 'sub-editors,' who volunteered each to take charge of a letter or part of one, and by whom the slips were in turn further arranged, classified, and to some extent used as the basis of definitions and skeleton schemes of the meanings of words in preparation for the Dictionary. The editorship of the work as a whole was undertaken by the late Mr. Herbert Coleridge, whose lamented death on the very threshold of his work

6. James Murray's 1879 Appeal to readers to read books for the *OED* in order to gather illustrative quotations

7. A 'slip' used in making the first edition of the _Oxford English Dictionary_

The guiding principles of the _OED_ had been carefully outlined in two influential lectures given to the London Philological Society in 1857. As the philologist and theologian Richard Chenevix Trench here explained, dictionary-making in English was, in a number of ways, now to reject what had gone before. The lexicographer was henceforth to be a historian not a critic. The remit was, moreover, to be inclusivity, not selection of those words which, for whatever reasons, might be seen as 'good' or worth recording. And the dictionary was itself to be redefined as an 'inventory' – a full record of the language as it was actually used.

The rise of large scholarly dictionaries is, of course, only one strand of lexicographical history at this time. If words, as conceived by Passow, simply 'tell their own story', a range of competing narratives in fact intervene in the kinds of stories which would, in reality, emerge across the 19th century. Noah Webster's work in America provides a particularly important example. Webster's work from the beginning deliberately engaged with very different narratives to those which had been articulated in earlier English dictionaries. The political dependence of 'our American colonies' had, for instance, been embedded within evidence used in Johnson's earlier entry for *reddle* (which he defined as 'a sort of mineral').

In 1828, however, Webster, in keeping with a now independent nation (and a very different stage of history), crafted an equally independent *American Dictionary of the English Language*. 'It is not only important, but in a degree necessary, that the people of this country, should have an *American Dictionary* of the English Language', he argued, here making another critical departure from the past. Webster's dictionary reflected a different material culture (*squash, racoon*) as well as different patterns of political understanding. 'No person in this country will be satisfied with the English definitions of the words *congress, senate* and *assembly*', he stated. Both history and nation had diverged: 'although these are words used in England, yet they are applied in this country to express ideas which they do not express in that country'. Just as Trench would note in his 1857 lectures, the dictionary is, in essence, a 'historical monument, the history of a nation seen from one point of view'.

Dictionaries and dictionary-making, as Webster's work attests, can therefore participate in patriotic resistance (and nationalist endeavour), prompting other interesting questions about which stories get told in dictionaries – and why. 'A great number of words in our language require to be defined in a phraseology accommodated to the condition and institutions of the people in these states, and the people of England must look to an American Dictionary for a correct understanding of such terms', Webster firmly contended in 1828. The same principles would, in time, come to operate for Australian English and Canadian English, New Zealand English, or Canadian French. 'Telling the story', as Chapter 5 will further explore, was not necessarily to be as simple as Passow – and Trench – had envisaged.

Dictionaries and the digital age

Another revolution lay in wait in the 20th century. Paper and postage, as we have seen, dominated the making of the *OED*; 'slips' were sent in from all over the world. Urgent communications with co-editors (at work in different parts of Oxford) were by bicycle. Émile Littré in France likewise laboriously assembled 415,636 sheets of paper on which his dictionary was written by hand. Modern dictionaries instead draw on corpora – vast, computerized databases, containing millions of words, across a wide range of sources, which can be analysed with far greater speed, rigour, and sophistication.

The transformations which computers have brought to dictionaries and dictionary-making can scarcely be underestimated – changing the scale of the data that can be analysed, as well as the ways in which lexicographers now work, and, as indicated in Chapter 1, the forms in which dictionaries and entries can now appear. For John Sinclair, one of the pioneers of corpus lexicography in Britain in the 1980s, the effect of the digital age on dictionary-making was akin to that which telescopes had upon astronomy. Sinclair's work on COBUILD (the Collins Birmingham University International Language Database) – and the resulting *Collins Cobuild English Language Dictionary* (a dictionary for language learners first published in 1987) – would, for example, place new and vital emphasis on the import of quantitative analysis, of frequency statistics for the use of different forms or meanings, and of the patterned nature of language in use.

The corpus – rather than a file of quotations – took centre stage. In this sense, a corpus, as here defined by Sinclair, was 'a collection of pieces of language text in electronic form, selected according to external criteria to represent, as far as possible, a language or language variety as a source of data for linguistic research'. Removing the limitations of a file of headwords, this consists of hundreds of millions of words of running text. The Oxford English Corpus (which includes data on English in use across the world), for instance, currently contains over two billion words – which can be sorted at the click of a key and on a range of parameters. As Sinclair already recognized in the 1980s, the corpus as a tool for lexicography provided a depth and flexibility of data which earlier dictionary-makers had clearly lacked. Open-ended corpora – such as the Cobuild corpus (now known as the Bank of English) – are, moreover, like language itself, dynamic rather than static. The 20 million words originally analysed by Sinclair had, by 2007, increased to 450 million words, and by 2010, to over 650 million.

It is the corpus too that is able to provide precise information on currency, on sense differentiation, and which importantly underpins the nature of the definitions that are written. Bilingual as well as vernacular dictionaries draw on this shift of methodology. As the editors of the *Oxford Hachette French Dictionary* stress, for example, it is the 'vast electronic databanks of English and French, both written and spoken' which 'shapes every dictionary entry … highlighting important constructions, illustrating difficult meanings, and focusing attention on common usage'. Even more important is the stress now placed on the representativeness of the corpus – the criteria by which a corpus is designed to represent real language in use (and evidence of this). Sinclair, for example, firmly excluded poetry (a staple of Johnson's evidence and also widely used in the *OED*) from his work on COBUILD. Instead, as Figure 8 illustrates, the modern corpus presents a striking image of contemporary discourse, deriving from sources such as newspapers, magazines, leaflets, and conversations, weblogs, radio, and television.

For Sinclair, it was this reorientation in the nature and history of the dictionary that lay at the heart of what he envisaged as 'progressive lexicography'. As he noted, this was to be a process in which the dictionary acts as

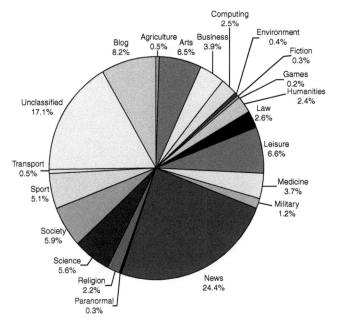

8. The composition of the Oxford English Corpus

a device through which the user will observe the living language.
Not the frozen fillets of the printed citations, nor the stuffed dummies
of the made-up examples, but the language as it is when it is being
used.

The corpus revolution will be discussed in more detail in the
following chapter, especially in terms of the changing craft of
lexicography, and the implications for how dictionaries are to be
both researched and written. What is abundantly clear, however,
is the way in which 'real authentick history' is now firmly
embedded in the living language as used across a wide range of
contexts. Against the images of a static language which

41

preoccupied a considerable part of earlier lexicography (and indeed, writing on language more generally), modern lexicography is, in a variety of ways, instead enthusiastically engaged in tracking ongoing history in a firm commitment to both language and language change, and to spoken as well as written forms.

Chapter 3
Craft

'I know of no more enjoyable intellectual activity than working on a dictionary', wrote the American lexicographer James Hulbert in 1955. His words radiated a sense of quiet contentment. If 'every day one is confronted by new problems', these are 'usually small, but absorbingly interesting'. Lexicography, he noted, 'does not make one's life anxious, nor build up hopes only to have them collapse'. And at the end of the day, 'one feels healthily tired'. Other lexicographers have, however, expressed rather different views. '*To make dictionaries is* dull *work*', Samuel Johnson announced, providing an illustrative sentence for his eighth sense of *dull* (defined as 'not exhilaterating; not delightful'). His preface was still more expansive. Dictionary-making was characterized in terms of demerit rather than delight, condemned as 'drudgery for the blind', 'the proper toil of artless industry' – a craft which requires the capacity to bear 'burthens with dull patience' and to beat 'the track of the alphabet with sluggish resolution'.

Johnson's words form part of a larger tradition, a narrative of toil and weariness which often featured in dictionary prefaces. The *lacrimae lexicographi*, or the 'tears of the lexicographer', was the point at which the human cost of lexicography was made plain, stressing the dedication (and desolation) that dictionary-making involved. It involved 'much more laboure and paines, than ye can possibly thinke', Peter Levens stated of his English and Latin dictionary of 1570. 'Searching words for a Dictionarie' was the 'most vnprofitable and vnpleasant task', John Minsheu declared in 1599 after completing his *Dictionarie in Spanish and English*; a 'good deal of time and paines' had been spent 'bringing the words into the Alphabet', he added. 'The mere study of the result, arranged in some degree of order, gives little idea of the toil and difficulties encountered', James Murray similarly affirmed in the first part of the *OED*. Murray's private letters were still more revealing, lamenting working days of 18 hours in which the dictionary is 'a great abyss that will never cry "Enough!"'.

Architecture

Extant archival material for both the *OED* and Johnson's dictionary allows us to examine – as we will see – some of the ways in which they were slowly assembled, built up piece by piece. As contemporary reviews confirm, such works were often referred to as 'monuments' or 'edifices', likened to human constructions such as St Paul's Cathedral or the Egyptian pyramids. The idea of dictionaries as, in some way, analogous to large and complex buildings was, in fact, apposite in a number of ways. Size and planning, for example, are of vital importance, whether for what is known as the *macrostructure* of the dictionary (the overall wordlist of an individual work – and how big this is to be, including too considerations of its overarching design, including front-matter and end-matter) or for the *microstructure* (the information that is, in a variety of ways, provided about each headword). Data provide the foundations, lending support to the entries which will subsequently be built up.

As for buildings, intended use (and users) also play a part, while scale and cost need to be carefully aligned. The more space taken up, the greater the expense will be. More words and senses demand more time (which also has cost implications, whether the dictionary in question is digital or print). The fact that different editors can incline to being 'lumpers' or 'splitters' (or, in other words, to packaging senses up together, or to unpicking them in fine – perhaps over-fine – detail) will present other areas of delicate negotiation. Selection – in ways that have wide-ranging implications for the eventual shape of any given dictionary – remains inevitable.

Each element is therefore the product of countless moments at which decisions must be taken. Pronunciation (and the kind of transcriptions to be used), spelling, etymology, definition, sense division, sense ordering (earliest sense first or most common sense first?), and the range, type, or scale of evidence, will all demand painstaking attention. Fifty-eight different spellings of *corroboree* ('An Aboriginal dance ceremony, of which song and rhythmical musical accompaniment are an integral part'), for example, confronted the editors of the *Australian National Dictionary* in the mid-1980s. Only one could be given as a headword. Richard Allsopp faced similar difficulties in editing the 1996 *Dictionary of Caribbean English Usage*. 'What spelling shall be determined (and by whom) for items nationals never bothered to spell until now that they need to write them?', he demanded, faced with the task of creating a reference model for spelling as well as meaning. Systematic planning was vital.

Even features which, to the casual user, seem relatively trivial – such as the choice of fonts and font size or the distribution of white space on a page – can be equally problematic in building the dictionary. 'Hours, days, months are spent examining sample pages, column width, typeface, type size, space between lines, the size of the margins, and so on', Robert Chapman, an editor with experience on a wide range of American dictionaries, confirms. Nothing in a dictionary is, or should be, accidental. Both architecture and foundations are, at best, the results of careful and considered thought.

Time and change

Dictionaries, at their most basic, consist of a list of words and meanings. How this list is arrived at, and how the subsequent analysis of meaning takes place, is, however, as we will see, a matter of considerable diversity in itself. Any consideration of lexicography as craft, for instance, inevitably confronts us with a pattern of extraordinary change. If the medieval lexicographer began his task with a stylus and some handmade manuscript, it is the keyboard (and keyboarding), the workstation and screen, as well as vast resources of electronic data, which dominate dictionary-making today. 'Lexicography without computerized corpus data is practically unthinkable nowadays', writes William Meijs. Databases and software, computerized concordances and frequency statistics as well, of course, as the salience of the corpus, all testify to processes which differ markedly from those of the past. *Computation*: 'Reckoning or casting up Accounts', Nathaniel Bailey stated in his highly popular *Universal Etymological English Dictionary* in 1721. A *computist*, Johnson confirmed, was 'one skilled in the art of numbers or computation'. As here, early dictionary entries can eloquently act as witnesses to the pre-digital age.

Craft can, in earlier dictionaries, seem to belong to another world. It has, for instance, often been depicted in terms of the crafty – depending less on independent research and data than on a process of unwitting collaboration or piracy. Narratives of this kind underpin the accusations levelled at Phillips by Blount (and discussed in Chapter 2) or – in another famous spat in terms of lexicographical history – those directed at Joseph Worcester by Noah Webster. An assistant on Webster's 1828 *American Dictionary of the English Language*, Worcester had in the process – at least so Webster contended – been appropriating words and definitions for the *Comprehensive Pronouncing and Explanatory English Dictionary* which Worcester published two years later. The 'dictionary wars' that ensued ran across much of the 19th century, dividing the allegiance of readers and reviewers between the Anglocentric Worcester – for whom British English was 'more harmonious and agreeable' – or the lexicographical independence Webster instead firmly proclaimed.

Cutting and pasting were, for Webster, seen therefore as firmly physical processes as they applied to dictionary-making. 'A chief qualification for authorship is a dextrous use of an inverted pen, and a pair of scissors', he scathingly commented.

Turning a quill pen upside down converts it into a very good brush for applying glue – and an effective tool in appropriating material plundered from other works. Craft here can seem uncomfortably close to plagiarism. Conversely, as Sidney Landau has argued, 'A really new dictionary would be a dreadful piece of work, missing innumerable basis words and senses, replete with absurdities and unspeakable errors.' These tensions run through the earlier history of dictionaries. Did dictionary-makers write or compile dictionaries? If they compiled them, did this mean that craft was merely copying, taking entries and evidence from other sources as they saw fit? Even Webster crafted his own dictionary with a copy of Johnson before him. Johnson likewise worked with a copy of Bailey, as well as a range of other texts.

Appropriation and apprenticeship

Like a form of apprenticeship, it is clear that all lexicographers necessarily learn from what has gone before. If we examine the craft of dictionary-making carefully, it is evident that earlier dictionaries provide important models – of what is, and what is not, to be done. Considered study of the kind of words or senses included can, for instance, act as a spur for the kinds of decisions taken in later works. Such processes of decision-making can, moreover, reveal deliberate departures as much as conscious continuities. Precedents can be observed – but also changed, extended, and recrafted in ways which impact on both micro- and macrostructure.

Craft, seen in this light, is cumulative. 'I borow'd what I thought for my purpose, and follow'd 'em where I safely might', as the anonymous compiler of the *Glossographia Anglicana Nova*, published in 1707, noted of his own patterns of strategic assimilation. 'I did not think my self oblig'd to stumble after them because I follow'd them', he added. Giuseppi Baretti, a friend of Johnson, and the editor of a range of 18th-century bilingual – and bidirectional – dictionaries in English, Italian, and Spanish, was explicit on the benefits that a considered engagement with previous work could bring. 'The latest Dictionaries of any language are generally the best', he argued, since 'the last editor must be very injudicious, should he not retain whatever appears to be valuable in former works of the like nature'. Moreover, any 'diligent and skilful' editor should be able to 'insert what has been omitted by preceding lexicographers'. A 'moderate degree of judgement', meanwhile, guided decisions on any forms that should now be omitted. Webster's use of Johnson can equally be seen in this light; entries and evidence were scrutinized, while, as we might expect, new material – based in American usage and American writing – was introduced in line with his ambitions to create a distinctively *American Dictionary*.

Even before the return to first principles which was to be emphasized by 19th-century philology, it is clear that primary research into new words or meanings could also be important. Nevertheless, deducing the working methods of the past in this respect can be challenging, requiring detective work in possible or probable sources. The fact that, say, words used by the lexically inventive poet Thomas Nashe – such as *assertionate* ('to avouch') and *anthropophagize* ('one man to kill and eat anothers flesh') – occur in Cockeram's *English Dictionarie* of 1623 convincingly suggests, for instance, that Nashe was used as a source while Cockeram was collecting material for his own work.

Prefaces to individual dictionaries also reveal information of value. We know from the preface of Sir Thomas Elyot's *Dictionarie* of

1538 that he was offered books from Henry VIII's library when in fact just over halfway through his first draft (at which point, he returned to the beginning of the alphabet, adding new words and senses with the new information now at his disposal). Blount's preface to his *Glossographia* of 1656 likewise relates the ways in which his sense of being 'gravelled' (or overwhelmed) by new words prompted his subsequent collection of material – such indeed as *chocolate* (discussed in Chapter 1), or the equally new *coffa* [coffee]: 'Thought good and wholesome; they say it expels melancholy, purges choler, begets mirth, and [is] an excellent concoction', the *Glossographia* explained.

While Blount encountered words such as these in use by tradesmen in the capital, he also turned to contemporary writers (as well as other dictionaries) as further sources of information. A range of writers are explicitly referred to in his dictionary – Francis Bacon under *compendium*, Sir Thomas Browne's *Vulgar Errors* under *falcation* ('a mowing or cutting with Bill, or hook'), the religious writer and cleric Jeremy Taylor under *cognoscible* ('that may be known or enquired into'). As Blount makes plain, evidence was already seen as important in authenticating usage so that, for words such as these, 'I may not be thought the innovator of them'.

Blount's *Glossographia* can therefore reveal a number of elements at work within earlier dictionary-making. Craft – here in terms of the collection of data, the choice of a wordlist – is, however, already moving in certain directions rather than others. Reading, where this was done for the purposes of a dictionary, already tended to involve particular kinds of prestigious writing rather than engaging with the ordinary and colloquial – the kind of usages that, in other words, might be more typical or representative of the 'real English' of the Renaissance.

The crosscurrents of lexicography across Europe were also significant. Italian lexicography had, for example, early established important precedents in this respect; the proper territory of the dictionary-maker, as in Fabrizio Luna's *Vocabulario*, published in Naples in 1536, was located in the '*tre corone*', or the three crowns of Dante, Petrarch, and Boccaccio. Academy dictionaries crystallized this literary bias, informing too (as we have seen) popular perceptions of the dictionary as an essentially normative tool, teaching 'right language' through good writing – and examples of this. The work of the French-born Abel Boyer (1667–1729), author of a number of immensely popular bilingual dictionaries, offers another useful example. Good dictionary-making, Boyer stressed, requires 'industrious Care and Labour' – and a 'constant perusal of the best English authors' in order to document the 'Richness and Copiousness' of language. Like Blount, he cited a range of recent writers ('the great masters of the English tongue') as sources for particular words. Words 'found in any Writer of unsufficient Authority', Boyer added, are marked as 'Dubious'.

The dictionary-maker at work: Samuel Johnson

Gathering material for a dictionary is clearly a critical point in its making. We can usefully turn here to Samuel Johnson, a writer who enables us to engage far more closely with the principles and practices of earlier lexicography. Importantly, we have not only Johnson's 34-page *Plan of a Dictionary of the English Language* (1747), which sets out what he intended to do in writing a dictionary, and his 1755 Preface, which probes the reality of what he had in fact achieved, but also a number of the books Johnson read and annotated as he set about his task. Taken from his own bookshelves or borrowed from his friends (and often returned, as his biographer James Boswell records, 'so defaced as to be scarce worth owning'), these enable us to glimpse empirical engagement – and patterns of selection – at first hand.

Figure 9 is taken from the 1676 edition of *The Anatomy of Melancholy* by Robert Burton, one of the 'writers of the first reputation' in which, for Johnson, evidence and quotations were

THese Concupifcible and Irafcible Appetites are as the two twifts of a rope, mu-
tually mixt one with the other, and both
twining about the Heart : both good, as Auftin holds *l. 14. c. 9. de civ. Dei* : if they be
moderate : both pernitious if they be exorbitant. This Concupifcible appetite, howfo-
ever it may feem to carry with it a fhew of
pleafure and delight, and our concupifcences
moft part affect us with content and a pleaf-
ing object, yet if they be in extreams, they
rack and wring us on the other fide. A
true faying it is, *Defire hath no reft :* is infi-
nite in it felf, endlefs : and as ᵐ one calls it,
a perpetual rack, ⁿ or horfe-mill , according
to *Auftin* , ftill going round as in a ring.

*¹ Bonæ fi
rectam ra-
tionem fe-
quuntur,
malæ fi ex-
orbitant.*

*ᵐ Tho. Buo-
vie. Prob.
18.*

*ⁿ Molam
afinariam.*

9. Samuel Johnson's annotated copy of Robert Burton's *Anatomy of Melancholy* (1676), showing words underlined for potential inclusion in the dictionary

primarily to be sought. Johnson's methods, as this image
illustrates, were based in active reading and a personal scrutiny
of the text. As in the dictionary of the Accademia della Crusca
(and in an important extension of dictionary-making in English
in which quotations had been used in very limited ways), Johnson
decided to include illustrative citations for the majority of words
and senses in the dictionary. Burton's *Anatomy* was read with
this in mind, and we can see Johnson's dictionary-making at
work in his underlining of words such as *twists* in line 2 and, in
line 7, *concupiscible* (defined in the dictionary as 'impressing
desire; eager; desirous'). A range of words such as *profuse*,
dilate, *predicament*, and *oligarchy* are underlined on other
pages. The first letter of the potential headword was also noted
in the adjacent margin (the quotations were subsequently copied
out by one of Johnson's assistants).

We can see a clear process of selection (and rejection) at work. *Horse-mill* (visible in the penultimate line of the image) is not underlined and is thereby removed from consideration for the dictionary. Johnson also decided not to mark *dizard*, a word used later in Burton's text. The relevant entry in the dictionary (*Dizzard*: 'a blockhead; a fool') would be included without any supporting evidence; here, Johnson erroneously labelled it a 'dictionary word', one he had not found in use. Craft is, we could argue, clearly far from systematic at this date. As Johnson noted, information was 'gleaned as industry or chance should offer it'. Based on what he described as 'fortuitous and unguided excursions into books', his reading enabled him to assemble a citation file (an ordered collection of quotations). This was, however, self-evidently not a corpus in the modern sense. Rather than a set of intentionally balanced sources, Shakespeare, Milton, Dryden, Pope, and Addison, as well as the Bible, provide a considerable portion of Johnson's evidence. Burton, scarcely a representative writer for language in 1755, appears 16 times. Conversely, few contemporary quotations appear.

The notion of data collection as a 'fortuitous ... excursion', moreover, rendered gaps and inaccuracies inevitable. If we look at Johnson's wordlist, we can see that *athlete* was omitted while *athletick* was not. *Amorphous*, included in Bailey (which, as we have seen, Johnson read while writing his own work), was also dropped. The nature of available evidence can also compromise the information the dictionary provides. *Jeopardy*, Johnson states, is 'not now in use' – though, as a later entry reveals, he would himself use it in defining *peril* ('danger; hazard; jeopardy'). Memory – rather than the modern insistence on the verification, and absolute accuracy, of data – could introduce additional errors. Quotations attributed to Milton can derive from Pope; likewise, as in the illustration below, the 'same' quotation from *Hamlet* appears for both *distilment* (the correct reading) and *instilment* in the fourth edition of Johnson's dictionary in 1773.

DISTI'LMENT. *n.s.*

[from *distil.*]

That which is drawn by distillation. A word formerly used, but now obsolete.

> Upon my secure hour thy uncle stole,
> And in the porches of mine ears did pour
> The leperous *distilment.*
> > *Shakespeare's Hamlet.*

INSTI'LMENT._n.s.
[from *instil.*]

Any thing instilled.
> The leperous *instilment.*
> > *Shakespeare.*

We can also see considerable advances. The wealth of evidence which Johnson had assembled – over 114,000 quotations were included in the finished text of 1755, though he clearly had even more at his disposal – meant, for example, that meaning and sense division could be examined in considerable detail. Quotations, as Johnson stressed, were his 'authorities'; most words and senses are accompanied by evidence of this kind. As a result, the precedents offered by earlier English dictionaries are deliberately transcended. Bailey, in his *Universal Etymological Dictionary* of 1721, had, for instance, defined *dull* as 'heavy, sluggish, stupid'. Johnson instead carefully anatomized it in 10 separate senses, most supported by citational evidence. He set out 68 sense divisions for *to go* (making particular advances in the treatment of phrasal verbs such as *go out, go over*). The corresponding entry in Bailey had simply stated 'to walk, move, &c'. Craft became a far more ambitious activity as Johnson strove to calibrate the nuances and associations that made up individual elements of meaning.

DULL. *adj.*

[*dwl*, Welsh; *dole*, Saxon; *dol*, mad, Dutch.]

1. Stupid; doltish; blockish; unapprehensive; indocile; slow of understanding.

> Such is their evil hap to play upon *dull* spirited men.
>
> *Hooker.*

> He that hath learned no wit by nature, nor art, may complain of gross breeding, or comes of a very *dull* kindred.
>
> *Shak.*

> Sometimes this perception, in some kind of bodies, is far more subtile than the sense; so that the sense is but a *dull* thing in comparison of it.
>
> *Bacon's Natural History.*

> Every man, even the *dullest*, is thinking more than the most eloquent can teach him how to utter.
>
> *Dryden.*

2. Blunt; obtuse.

> Meeting with time, Slack thing, said I,
> Thy scythe is *dull*; whet it, for shame.
>
> *Herbert.*

3. Unready; aukward.

> Gynecia a great while stood still, with a kind of *dull* amazement looking stedfastly upon her.
>
> *Sidney.*

> O help thou my weak wit, and sharpen my *dull* tongue.
> *Fairy Queen, b. i. stanz. 2.*

> Memory is so necessary to all conditions of life, that we are not to fear it should grow *dull* for want of exercise, if exercise would make it stronger.
>
> *Locke.*

4. Hebetated; not quick.

This people's heart is waxed gross, and their ears are *dull* of hearing.

Bible Math, xiii. 15.

5. Sad; melancholy.

6. Sluggishly; heavy; slow of motion.

Thenceforth the waters waxed *dull* and slow,

And all that drunk thereof did faint and feeble grow. *F. Q.*

7. Gross; cloggy; vile.

She excels each mortal thing

Upon the dull earth dwelling.

Shak. Two Gent. of Verona.

8. Not exhilaterating; not delightful; as, *to make dictionaries is dull work.*

9. Not bright; as, *the mirror* is dull, *the fire is* dull.

I'll not be made a soft and dull ey'd fool,

To shake the head, relent, and sigh, and yield

To Christian intercessors.

Shakespeare's Merch. of Venice.

10. Drowsy; sleepy.

Even so, the nature of a 'good' definition could remain problematic. 'To interpret a language by itself is very difficult', Johnson admitted. If earlier dictionaries provided 'hard' words with 'easy' definitions, Johnson can sometimes seem determined to do the opposite. A *mill* is 'an engine or fabrick' in which corn is 'comminuted', a process aided by *mill-cogs* which are themselves defined by their 'denticulations'. Here we can need a dictionary to understand the proffered explanation. The monosyllabic *rust* is defined as 'the red desquamation of old iron'. The fact that *desquamation* was defined as 'the act of scaling foul bones' did not help.

Knowing how much information to give could be equally problematic. Johnson's definition of *umbrella*, for example, fails to specify that it is an object that is held ('a skreen used in hot countries to keep off the sun, and in others to bear off the rain'); his definition of *fur* ('Soft hair of beasts found in cold countries, where nature provides coats suitable to the weather') inadvertently suggests that creatures elsewhere are hairless. Other definitions simply perplex, as in *wade*: 'To pass water without swimming'. Still others reveal the superimposed opinion of the dictionary-maker, irrespective of the evidence that might be provided.

Here too, as we will see, craft would be cumulative, a process of learning what not to do. Modern lexicography demands greater transparency, as well as explicitness. 'The definer must put himself in the place of someone who hasn't the vaguest idea what the word means and try to anticipate the wrong assumption', Landau stresses. Definitions must not be more complex than the thing defined, nor should closed loops of meaning be created, as in Johnson's entries for *hind* ('the she to the stag') and *stag* ('the male of the hind').

Science and systematicity: gathering the raw materials

For Johnson, lexicography was seen as an art. Craft in the 19th and 20th centuries tended, however, to place lexicography firmly among the sciences. Empiricism and an intentionally scientific engagement with facts led, as Chapter 2 has indicated, to a number of significant shifts in both the conception – and the underlying methods – of dictionary-making. The kind of individual and *ad hoc* reading by which Johnson and Blount had gathered evidence was displaced by schemes of collective endeavour – enabling the collection of information from a wide range of texts, literary and non-literary, on a scale hitherto impossible.

This wide-ranging and first-hand engagement with evidence clearly transformed the quantity of material available for the dictionary-maker. James Murray, for example, noted that he had 20 yards of material for words in H, and another 17 for those in I. Nevertheless, systematicity – and the problem of knowing enough about language – could remain challenging. Volunteer readers, however enthusiastic, are, in many ways, as Murray recognized, merely unskilled labour. If they provide a wealth of valuable evidence in terms of scale, they can also miss the obvious. Murray found he had over 50 examples for the comparatively rare *abusion* ('misuse, misapplication, perversion') but fewer than 5 illustrating *abuse*. Other common words such as *bedspread* were missed altogether (it first entered the *OED* in the 1933 *Supplement*). In contrast, unusual literary words such as *lin-lan-lone*, coined by the poet Alfred Tennyson to represent a chime of three bells, were spotted immediately.

Craft

That dictionary-making should engage with representativeness – reflecting the facts of language as it was in fact used – was nevertheless seen as increasingly important. 'The question that should concern the lexicographer is not, should the word be in the English language? but *is* it? Is the word used; and, if so, in what sense is it used?', as Isaac Funk stressed in America in his *Standard Dictionary of the English Language* in 1893: 'A dictionary is expected primarily to tell what words and phrases mean as used by representative writers and speakers of the language.' How exactly this was to be determined would, however, long remain problematic. As Murray had argued, for instance, only if lexicographers had full concordances – complete listings of every word – for every publication of whatever type would they really be able to ensure that the data in their possession were sufficiently robust. Evidence from speech, he added, presented other difficulties – words were often used for 20 or 30 years before they emerged in print. But how was evidence of this kind to be located, and indeed recorded? The gaps in the data seemed insurmountable.

Dictionary-making across much of the 20th century would continue to explore these problems of data and data collection. Nevertheless – even before the advent of computers – a number of important trends and developments can be detected. One is the ever-increasing emphasis on the range of sources that must be considered by the dictionary-maker. The editors of Merriam-Webster's 1934 *New International Dictionary of the English Language*, for example, emphasize the 'many thousands of books, pamphlets, magazines, newspapers, catalogues, and learned, technical, and scientific, periodicals' which had been scrutinized. 'It cannot be emphasized too strongly that the reason for the fundamental and thorough soundness of the Merriam-Webster Dictionary is that it is a "Citation Dictionary"', they affirm. Canonical and non-canonical sources exist side by side. Displacing the 'best writers' who appear on Johnson's title page, the evidence of ephemeral productions such as catalogues and newspapers, pamphlets and periodicals assumes prominence, moving both dictionary-maker and dictionary-user closer to the kind of documentation of 'real' usage that descriptive principles had long desired.

Technological shift in other ways also solved some of the concerns earlier voiced by Murray. Spoken evidence, for instance, was particularly vital for languages and language varieties which, for a range of reasons, did not possess the kind of lengthy written history which characterizes, say, standard English. The gathering of evidence on Jamaican English in the 1950s – the groundwork for what would become the *Dictionary of Jamaican English*, edited by Frederic Cassidy and Robert le Page – required fieldwork and face-to-face research. While transcription – and lengthy questionnaires – were important, so too was the ability to collect evidence directly from speech. Cassidy, for example, travelled round Jamaica equipped with a reel-to-reel tape recorder (which weighed 40 pounds and required a 25-pound converter). Citations were spoken, deriving from schoolchildren, fishermen, teachers, and boat-builders rather than 'great writers'. Both dictionary and dictionary-maker were brought much closer to the primacy of speech.

Fieldwork likewise provided the basis for the *Dictionary of American Regional English*. Information on words and usage was laboriously gathered in the late 1960s from over 1,000 communities across all 50 states: 80 fieldworkers, travelling in what were popularly known as 'Word Wagons', engaged with a kind of hands-on lexicographical endeavour that was strikingly remote from the 'armchair lexicography' of which Johnson and other early lexicographers were often accused. The resulting wordlist smacked of the colloquial and idiomatic, as in words such as *upscuddle*, 'a noisy quarrel, a disturbance', used in the Appalachians; or New England *whop over*, 'to collapse, tumble over'; or the evocative *catawampus*, a widely used adjective meaning 'askew, awry, wrong' – as a noun in the South, research also confirmed the latter's use in the sense 'an imaginary monster; a hobgoblin'.

Putting the raw materials to work

Gathering the raw materials is, of course, just one part of the problem. Deciding what to do with them can be even more difficult. Even if both the scale and scope of underlying material changed significantly from the mid-19th century onwards, this didn't necessarily mean that writing dictionaries became easier. One could, in fact, argue that the opposite was true.

We could, for instance, look at the kind of difficulties faced by James Murray as, using the piles of assembled quotations, he tried to establish exactly what *handsome* might be said to mean. As he wrote to Fitzedward Hall, one of the valuable volunteer helpers on the dictionary, this 'is a desperately difficult word to grasp'. Indeed, he confessed, 'none of us quite agree in our notion of the actual sense of "handsome" '. More to the point, he added, 'I find it impossible to formulate the differences between current & many obsolete senses, and between British and many American uses, exc[ept] by saying "I should say this," and "I should not say that"'. 'If you can send us a definition', Murray urged Hall, 'it shall be lovingly considered.'

Facts, as here, have to be interpreted, while even the existence of ample evidence does not necessarily indicate the right way to take. Evidence had to be sorted and classified, divided into preliminary divisions, and then progressively split into senses and subsenses, common combinations, or compound forms. As for *handsome*, as Murray's private letters reveal, at what point one sense became distinct from another could be difficult to determine, open to conflicting judgements on the part of different editors or subeditors. Behind the rhetoric of science, therefore, lie potential subjectivities – how many senses actually exist, and how many can be included, given additional considerations of expense? How should definitions be phrased – not least since using one word rather than another will, in turn, potentially shift the nuances to be conveyed? Who, moreover, will get the last word in such complex processes of decision-making?

Extant proof sheets from the first edition of the *OED* offer other snapshots of the tortuous process by which definition could be arrived at. As Figure 10 shows, here for the humble word *louse*, a web of crossing-out, rewriting, and revision characterizes craft at this stage. Was a *louse* 'an apterous insect of the genus *Pediculus*, parasitic on human beings and animals, esp. in the hair, on which it deposits its nits and eggs', as the definition in the first proof states? Or was it, as a set of annotations in the margin instead declares, better defined as 'A parasitic insect ... infesting the human hair and skin and causing great irritation by its presence ...'? Changes in supporting evidence are clear at the

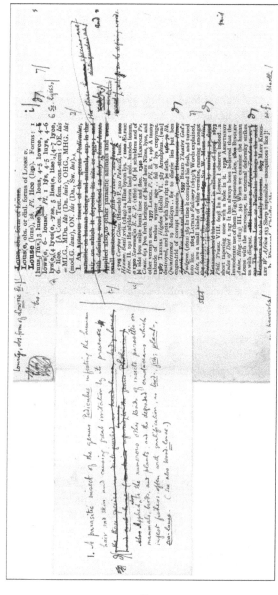

61

10. Behind the scenes revision on the proof sheets of the first edition of the *Oxford English Dictionary*, here for the word *louse*

same point; a 1561 citation from the early medical writer John Hollybush is deleted, together with those from a range of other texts. The entry overall is shortened, tightened, and pruned. The difficulties of what to take out – and what to leave – are nevertheless conspicuous. A 1657 citation from the writer and politician Sir William Mure is first included, set in type, and then deleted by hand; then – as the marginal annotation 'stet' denotes – it was temporarily reprieved, only to disappear for good at a still later stage of revision; no trace of it appears in the published text.

Moreover, while it might be tempting to see craft of this kind as part of a long-gone past (Murray was battling *handsome* in the late 1890s, *louse* was being drafted just after 1900), a glance at the making of the *Australian National Dictionary* in the 1980s still offers salutary lessons. Here, filing cabinets (rather than the pigeonholes used by the *OED*) contained the assembled data; each piece of evidence was carefully inscribed on an index card and filed alphabetically. The endeavour to write entries was, as described by its editor, Bill Ramson, nevertheless like an 'elaborate game of patience'. Index cards were spread out over the floor of the office, sometimes for days. Amongst them sat the editor or subeditor, arranging and rearranging the material in the hope of seeing the vital patterns of sense division and development, word history and meaning. Only then could the entry be drafted, eventually emerging in the finished text.

The neatness of the finished text betrays, of course, little trace of the uncertainties and doubts that have to be countered before its final form can take shape. Ramson's image of craft as a game of patience here usefully reminds us of the potential randomness – and arbitrariness – dictionary-making can involve. There is, after all, no pre-ordained order to a dictionary entry, no absolute or automatic limit on how senses are to be divided – or indeed how many (and which) words are to be included. Franz Passow's idealized image of dictionaries in which words simply tell their own story does not quite match the truths which the realities of dictionary-making reveal. Craft – here seen as an active rather than passive process – necessarily shapes the form that each and every text assumes.

Craft and computers

It is the computer, of course, that has fundamentally transformed the craft of modern dictionary-making. 'No human reader can capture all the examples of how even one word is used in a single book, let alone in a hundred or a thousand books', stressed the editors of the *Oxford Hachette French Dictionary* (the first French and English dictionary to have been written using corpora): 'No human being, even with all the time in the world, can remember all the ways of using even one small word, let alone discover how other people use it.' Likewise, 'no human being can take ten thousand sentences and put them in alphabetical order of one of their words'. In corpus lexicography, these are all tasks that – using computers – can be accomplished in a few seconds. 'None of us would want to go back to the bad old days of editing dictionaries without a corpus to help us', the editors declare.

A modern electronic corpus, as we have seen in Chapter 2, consists of hundreds of millions of words of running text (and often more), organized with reference to a particular distribution of text-types and registers, and including speech as well as writing. Craft is necessarily very different, requiring also a very different array of people. If Johnson worked in an attic with, at various points, six amanuenses who copied out – by hand – the quotations he marked in books, modern lexicography involves software engineers and data-capture assistants, as well as editors or etymologists. Data is tagged to give an indication of field (e.g. science, news reporting, fiction, religion), of language variety (e.g. US English, GB English, South African English), as well as being tagged in linguistic ways (e.g. to indicate part of speech).

Engagement with typical language use is all-important. Context, rather than the word in isolation, is, however, now particularly salient. In a corpus, we are, for instance, no longer limited to the headword or phrase which a reader for a citation file might have chosen to give (and under which, written on an index card or 'slip', it was subsequently sorted and filed away). Corpora, based on running text rather than pre-specified headwords, are instead able to reveal patterned structures of usage across billions of words of data. Meaning – and its analysis – instead resides in what is termed *collocation*: 'the occurrence of two or more words within a short space of each other in a text' as this was defined by John Sinclair, one of the pioneers of corpus lexicography.

In other words, rather than looking at words in isolation, as in the processes of the past, the aim is, in essence, that of 'judging a word by the company it keeps' (a maxim based on the work of the linguist J. R. Firth). What is known as Key Word in Context (or KWIC) has therefore emerged as a fundamental element in corpus use and analysis, and across monolingual and bilingual lexicography. Corpus evidence on *handsome*, in Figure 11 from the Oxford English Corpus, swiftly reveals the greater flexibility of approach, and the advantages this can bring. Figure 12 shows, for example, a typical Key Word in Context concordance. *Handsome* appears centrally, framed by running text on either side (though, since a corpus is based on running text, these positions can be changed if we so wish; we can have more or less running text on either side as we probe context in more detail).

Information on frequency, which corpora readily provide, adds still more detail. As in Figure 12, frequency listings enable patterns of usage to be seen with striking ease and transparency. Certain patterns – *handsome* modifying male person, as in *hunk, gentleman, chap, fellow*; or *handsome* modifying quantity of money, as in *profit, dividend* – are more prominent. Others are rarer – perhaps surprisingly, for example, no collocations appear for *handsome woman*. Indeed, if we look at column 2, we can see

handsome new_oec_plus_biwec_alt freq = 21747

change c

X* mod N 14318 3.6		N is ADJ* 1494 11.2		ADV ADJ* 3321 21.7		V ADJ* 475 10.1		and/or 7294 4.3	
prince	163 6.93	he	858 6.18	ruggedly	100 9.83	look	374 2.75	tall	427 7.54
dividend	138 6.48	you	90 3.63	strikingly	88 8.48			charming	174 7.36
stranger	156 6.37	she	36 2.83	dashingly	26 7.96			dashing	35 6.8
hunk	34 5.84	they	50 2.05	impossibly	34 7.28			charismatic	64 6.69
gentleman	106 5.79	I	45 0.96	classically	25 7.15			well-built	22 6.44
devil	56 5.67			uncommonly	16 6.88			well-dressed	23 6.37
face	552 5.12	**ADJ* ADV 150 35.7**		exceedingly	35 6.84			dark-haired	19 6.15
profit	248 5.07	enough	134 4.14	conventionally	14 6.25			suave	21 6.14
visage	16 4.94	indeed	16 3.4	blandly	8 5.96			blond	36 6.08
chap	25 4.91			extraordinarily	26 5.91			virile	16 5.95
actor	173 4.87			undeniably	11 5.73			athletic	51 5.78
man	1728 4.87			remarkably	35 5.64			rugged	28 5.64
knight	26 4.79			ridiculously	14 5.62			dark	297 5.6
reward	64 4.74			exceptionally	23 5.59			Georgian	26 5.5
lad	45 4.74			incredibly	54 5.38			capacious	11 5.44
payoff	20 4.63			unusually	14 4.71			young	1133 5.44
brick	48 4.62			extremely	102 4.56			personable	12 5.4
mahogany	14 4.59			excessively	6 4.46			muscular	25 5.31
fellow	108 4.46			very	1050 4.4			slim	29 5.3
suitor	14 4.46			quite	160 3.99			intelligent	76 5.25
beau	11 4.42			rather	36 3.94			trim	13 5.24
edifice	14 4.41			wonderfully	7 3.84			strapping	10 5.22
sum	82 4.39			that	22 3.47			debonair	9 5.21
bachelor	16 4.29			equally	27 3.43			wealthy	60 5.15
fairground	10 4.28			particularly	52 3.33			witty	25 5.12

11. Screen shot of concordance for *handsome*, taken from the Oxford English Corpus

structures such as 'she is handsome' appear 36 times; the corresponding frequency for 'he is handsome' is 856.

The role of collocations in suggesting new patterns of meaning is particularly interesting. If we look at Figure 13, which shows a modern concordance for *carbon*, this indicates one meaning based, as we might expect, in its existence as a particular chemical element (as in collocations such as *radioactive carbon* or *lightweight carbon*). Careful scrutiny of other collocational patterns, in which *carbon* modifies words such as *footprint* or *emission* or *credit*, nevertheless suggests a splitting of sense in current usage. None of these collocations seems to fit with the first sense we examined. Instead, patterns of this kind can be used to

12. Screen shot of Key Word in Context for *handsome*, taken from the Oxford English Corpus

verify the use of *carbon* in the sense of 'carbon dioxide' (or other gaseous carbon compounds) as used in the context of greenhouse gases and global warming. *Carbon emission*, we might note, has a very high frequency score of 4,858, *carbon footprint* one of 888.

Important too is the statistical neutrality which information of this kind presents. If earlier dictionary-makers, as we have already seen in Chapter 1, could resort to negative value judgements when faced with a change in progress, factual information on frequency makes this kind of subjective resistance much more difficult, at least within the entries of the modern descriptive dictionary. Clearer too are decisions on the kind of labels a particular word or sense should be given. *Griefsome* was, for example, labelled obsolete during the writing of the first edition of the *OED*. A few months later, however, one of the editors used *griefsome* in drafting the carbon new_oec_plus_biwec_alt freq = 49669   change

V obj N*	1492 0.3	N* subj V	232 0.1	X mod N*	13392 1.1	X* mod N	46498 3.9	N* is ADJ	58 0.
sequester	52 8.8	occur	12 0.33	atmospheric	396 8.78	dioxide	12380 12.22	present	13 0.6
emit	53 6.45			inorganic	138 8.0	monoxide	3479 11.0		
store	100 5.31			organic	628 7.94	emission	4858 10.16		
absorb	51 4.86			nonfermentable	84 7.66	nanotube	850 9.11		
offset	12 3.7			photosynthetic	97 7.28	footprint	888 8.83		
extract	14 3.14			carbonyl	74 7.27	atom	1079 8.72		
dissolve	7 2.89			dissolve	193 7.21	fiber	1311 8.48		
capture	24 2.81			activate	183 6.89	poisoning	589 8.2		
fix	33 2.77			particulate	45 6.48	sequestration	377 7.97		
release	68 2.75			fermentable	37 6.47	isotope	406 7.85		
suck	7 2.64			cutting	118 6.1	dating	283 7.15		
lock	12 2.45			sole	108 6.1	sink	288 7.08		
accumulate	7 2.39			single-walled	27 6.03	tetrachloride	182 6.99		
contain	65 2.34			radioactive	42 5.75	copy	1031 6.88		
trap	7 2.18			net	132 5.71	assimilation	203 6.83		
incorporate	12 2.01			end-tidal	21 5.66	offset	179 6.81		
burn	13 1.78			assimilate	36 5.62	capture	218 6.56		
remove	27 1.51			elemental	23 5.41	steel	376 6.36		
reduce	35 1.13			terrestrial	31 5.37	trading	318 6.32		
supply	8 0.97			lightweight	35 5.33	metabolism	139 6.02		
produce	37 0.89			frozen	41 5.25	fork	125 6.0		
add	30 0.54			anthropogenic	17 5.23	flux	117 5.87		
save	10 0.14			man-made	25 5.23	fixation	108 5.79		
				greenhouse	51 5.17	credit	590 5.76		
				allochthonous	15 5.16	skeleton	106 5.67		

Craft

13. Screen shot of concordance for *carbon*, taken from the Oxford English Corpus

definition of *grievesomeness* ('the quality or condition of being griefsome', as a draft proof sheet still records). Here, intuition and usage failed to coincide; paradoxically *griefsome* was both obsolete (according to the label it had been given) and current (according to the usage of one of the editors). For the *OED*, in a pre-digital age, the problem was resolved, at least superficially, by omitting the definition. If this secured consistency, it was nevertheless at the expense of the facts of usage. The range of electronic databases available to a modern editor can, in contrast, quickly confirm that the ongoing usage of *griefsome* was by no means anomalous (and that the verdict of 'obsolete' was, at least at that point in lexical history, entirely unfounded).

The advent of the electronic corpus (as well as other electronic databases containing digital texts) therefore represents much more than a means by which data is realized in a different medium. Instead, corpus lexicography stresses the interconnectedness of words and meaning, and the importance of context and collocation in the ways in which meaning, usage, and sense division are analysed and understood. Bilingual lexicography can, in turn, rest not on just the presence of a lexicographer fluent in two languages, as in the early work of Abel Boyer, but on vast electronic databanks for both languages, on two corpora (each of hundreds of millions of words) which work in tandem, facilitating the analysis of equivalences and differences. The Bank of English in Collins dictionaries is hence matched by the Banque de Française Moderne or, in German, by the Deutsche Textbörse; information derives from radio and television programmes, business and personal correspondence, magazines and newspapers. The benefits for the dictionary-user – in terms of both understanding and production of the foreign language in question – are incalculable.

Nevertheless, lexicography itself remains a far from automated process. While the hand-written dictionary manuscripts of the past have disappeared, and editing is typically electronic and on screen, corpora are, of course, simply tools for the lexicographer to use. 'Computer-aided lexicography may have made the traditional means of collecting and marshalling evidence more efficient, and possibly more definitive, but essentially the task remains the same', Bill Ramson states. Determining the meaning of a word may therefore move in certain directions rather than others, guided by the information on frequency, the clustering of particular patterns, but intuition (and knowing what to look for) still play a part.

As in the witty definitions which feature in occasional entries in Chambers dictionaries (*comfort food*: 'mood-enhancing food that meets the approval of one's taste buds but not of one's doctor'; *channel-surf*: 'to switch rapidly between different channels in a forlorn attempt to find anything of interest'), users can still value a sense of pithy and personal engagement with meaning, one that is by no means constructed by computer. And as Chapter 5 will show, corpora – even if inscribed in databanks rather than personal selections from particular texts – can also reveal certain patterns of bias and ideological weighting that statistics cannot always exclude (and which might also need to be taken into consideration by the human lexicographer).

Statistics alone are not necessarily enough. Good definitions remain an art, a skill in encapsulating nuances of interpretation within a tightly organized form of words. The computer cannot, in reality, write the dictionary. As in the slogan with which Longman dictionaries currently define themselves, modern lexicography can in this respect be 'corpus-based' but not 'corpus-bound'.

Chapter 4
Authority

> Jerome began to mop up the wine with his paper napkin.
> 'I've always liked the notion of sequentiality.' ...
>
> 'Is sequentiality a word? I don't think it is.' Mira turned her
> head to one side and partly closed her eyes as she often did
> when she was questioning something. 'Perhaps we should
> look it up.'
>
> Jane Urquhart, *A Map of Glass* (2005)

Jane Urquhart's novel poses a conundrum. Does a word – or
indeed a meaning – exist because of its usage or because of its
existence in a dictionary? For Jerome, *sequentiality* offers a
meaningful and treasured notion, one which is both familiar and
familiarized. For Mira, *sequentiality* is instead placed in doubt
unless verified by the legitimizing authority which dictionaries are
assumed to wield. Jerome's authority is not enough. In this
narrative, it is the dictionary rather than the language which
sanctions and confirms. Usage, and users, are subordinate.

Images of authority, as we have seen in Chapter 1, are often firmly
entrenched in popular attitudes towards dictionaries. Authority,
however, offers its own conundrums. Looking at the *American
Heritage Dictionary*, authority is 'the power to enforce laws, exact
obedience, command, determine, or judge' as well as something

'invested with this power, especially a government or body of government officials'. It is also 'an accepted source of expert information or advice' (so that one can be an authority on a subject, such as music or physics). Other meanings range from 'the power to influence or persuade resulting from knowledge or experience', the 'confidence derived from experience or practice' (so that one can play the violin with authority), to the sense of 'justification; grounds', as in uses such as 'on what authority can this claim be made?'.

Authority, as this indicates, possesses a range of possible interpretations. It can suggest the authoritative or veer towards the authoritarian. It can characterize the factual and objective, or the very different territories of the opinionated and subjective. Its basis can be solid – or distinctly shaky. Attitudes to dictionaries, for those who make them as well as those who use them, can, as we will see, also participate in similar conflicts.

In Urquhart's novel, for example, the dictionary is clearly invested with a sense of power to which users should defer. We could nevertheless probe how this investment is made and on what it is based. Still more to the point is the problem of how, in practice, such authority is exercised or enforced. Where do its limits lie? As in Chapter 1, notions of a single legitimizing 'the dictionary' (and a single 'official' version of language) swiftly prove elusive in this respect. *Sequentiality* is not to be found in the 'Essential Edition' of, say, *Collins English Dictionary* (in which case, at least according to Urquhart's novel, Mira is right and Jerome must either rebel against the dictionary's authority or change his accustomed pattern of words). It does, however, appear in the earlier *Century Dictionary* ('The state of being sequential; natural connection and progress of thought, incident, or the like'), as well as in the *Random House Dictionary* – and indeed the *OED* – in which case, Jerome is off the hook and able to use *sequentiality* without fear of correction. As with many other aspects of

71

lexicography, elements that might seem simple, or even simplistic, can, on closer inspection, prove widely problematic.

Dictionaries and the sea of words

The nature of the relationships between dictionary, dictionary-makers, and language underpins a number of these complexities. Earlier writers, for example, often depicted language as a sea of words which the lexicographer must traverse – 'a sea more diuers, more dangerous, more stormie, and more comfortlesse than any Ocean', as John Florio stressed in his *World of Wordes*, a dictionary of Italian and English published in 1598. Metaphors of language as sea aptly give prominence to its ceaseless movement. Here, the role of the dictionary is that of a compass or guide, offering authoritative illumination against a tide of dark words, as well as a safe course through possibly unknown areas of vocabulary and meaning.

Narratives of lexicography that are significantly more interventionist appear elsewhere. Even in terms of the sea of words, the dictionary can be seen as something which provides not just illumination but an anchor, a work that might tether words and meanings in particular ways. The pages of a dictionary can evocatively seem to proffer a sense of stasis and stability, a way of resisting or countering the currents of change. Here, the image of authority is distinctly more powerful. Aims of this kind clearly informed proposals for an English dictionary as issued by the Royal Society in London in the 17th century. The Society established a committee with the explicit remit of 'improving the English language', while a 'Lexicon or Collection of all the pure English Words … so as no innovation might be us'd or favour'd' was proposed by John Evelyn (one of the Society's founding members). The role of both committee and dictionary was seen as firmly prescriptive. As the poet John Dryden (another member of the Royal Society) declared, a 'certain Measure' for both words and usage should be provided by a dictionary of this kind.

Though the Royal Society dictionary remained unrealized (and later campaigns for an English Academy, advanced by writers such as Jonathan Swift, also foundered), such proposals throw considerable light on the notion of authority as lexicographical ideal. Popular accounts of authority and the dictionary, for example, still often centre on the work of language academies and the ambitions of purism and linguistic control which these can promote. 'To work, with all possible care and diligence, to give our language definite rules and to make it pure, eloquent, and capable of dealing with art and science', as the original constitution of the Académie Française stated. 'It cleans, sets, and casts splendour', the original motto of the Spanish language academy, the Real Academia Española, likewise affirmed. In this image of language, authority clearly comes from outside usage. Reform and rule instead intentionally work together, crafting a new and improved mode of discourse.

Citizens and citizenship

Words which are seen as unwarranted lexical imports into a language can, for example, offer a particular focus for purism and control – especially when the form in question can already be expressed using the native resources of the language. Attempts by the Académie Française to reject loanwords such as *cocktail* in 1924 or *Yankee* in 1935 or, in modern French, to resist *chewing gum* or *é-mail* here all provide useful illustration. The endeavour to decide – and delimit – 'proper' usage in terms of words denoting electronic communication is, in this context, especially problematic. *É-mail* and *mél*, for example, are both resisted. *É-mail* – a blend deriving from English *electronic* and *mail* (the latter as characteristically used in North American English) – is, of course, conspicuously 'foreign'. For the Académie, this is firmly placed outside recommended usage (the existence in French of the form *email*, signifying 'enamel', can be seen as another factor in its disfavour).

The co-existing *mél* (a French blend deriving from *messagerie électronique*) – which can also be used in similar contexts – fares no better. It is formally restricted by the Académie to use as an abbreviation prefacing email addresses. Instead, the word *courriel* – another blend, though this time one that derives from *courrier électronique*, 'electronic mail', as used in Quebec French – was given the seal of authority by the Académie Française in 2003. Variation – and associated problems of acceptability – was thereby resolved, at least in principle. The non-native *é-mail* was denied linguistic citizenship, while *mél* and *courriel* were neatly consigned to distinct – and distinctive – territories of use.

We can see similar patterns at work in recommendations for the native *libre-service* (in place of English-derived *self-service*), for *franc-jeu* (versus English *fair play*), or for *la vacancelle* in place of *le weekend*. Official equivalents for anglicisms in the domains of computing are widely promoted: *le Réseau* versus *l'Internet*, *la Toile* versus *le Web*; *le publipostage* or *le pourriel* (itself a blend of *courriel* and *pourri*, meaning 'rotten') versus the loanword *le spam*. Here language can seem like a kind of nation-state in which territorial borders are closely monitored by the dictionary-maker. Issues of legitimate citizenship clearly cause concern, and loanwords judged undesirable or unnecessary are (at least intentionally) repatriated, being repelled over the borders of legitimate use.

New forms that arise as a result of internal creativity can, however, meet similar resistance (and not only, of course, from academies and the dictionaries that they produce). In France, the increasing use of 'feminized' forms for particular jobs presents a further useful example. Grammatical gender in constructions such as *le professeur* (the professor), *le juge* (the judge) has, for instance, traditionally dictated exclusively male reference (since both 'professor' and 'judge' are male nouns in French). Concerns about legitimacy – and the identity and use of 'proper' French – have in recent years nevertheless been prompted by the emergence of new and explicitly feminine forms such as *la professeure* and *la juge*. Arguably, of course, this change in language practice reflects changing social and cultural realities. Women (as well as men) are indeed judges or professors; *la chancelière*, the (female) chancellor, has likewise clearly attained currency following Angela Merkel's tenure of this role in Germany. Hitherto *une chancelière* denoted either the wife of a (male) chancellor, or was a noun that signified a type of foot-warmer.

Forms such as the feminine inflected *soldate* (alongside the uninflected male noun *soldat*, 'soldier') and *la professeure* (alongside masculine *le professeur*) – both of which were added to Oxford Language Dictionaries in 2008 – can, in this respect, be seen to reflect the changing facts of social history. A marked disinclination to accept the traditional meaning of *juge* as applied to women, in which it signified the 'wife of a (male) judge', is equally part of this pattern of change.

Nevertheless, the use of natural gender – rather than grammatical gender – in such instances clearly serves to challenge assumptions about the linguistic status quo. While French as spoken in Canada and Switzerland has widely embraced this process of 'feminization', and official language reviews in France have reached similarly liberal conclusions (job-title feminization was formally examined in 1998), the Académie – and its *Dictionnaire* – continue to express caution, as well as outright resistance at times. Correctness is set against usage, the authority of the academy against that of the language in use. Forms such as *la professeure* or *l'auteure* (a female author) are not, the academy rulings argue, linguistically justified since they conflict with established rules of derivation and inflection. Relevant forms are mentioned only to be dismissed.

French is not alone, of course, in expressing resistance to linguistic change of this kind. We could, for instance, usefully look at similar responses to the perceived 'illegitimate' extension of inflections in English. *Lesser*, as Johnson recorded in his dictionary, was 'A barbarous corruption of *less*, formed by the vulgar'. After all, to be *less* logically already involved a degree of comparison. The addition of the comparative suffix *-er* was, prescriptively, deemed redundant. The form was surely wrong.

Whether authority of this kind works in the real world is, of course, a different matter, especially when we come to consider what language users actually choose to do in their ordinary acts of speaking and writing. If, in modern French, the native *ordinateur* (rather than the proscribed loan *computer*) has indeed come to dominate in usage in this particular context, it is nevertheless clear that a range of other loans – as in *le spam*, alongside *spammer*, 'to spam', and indeed *le spamming*, with the *-ing* ending of the English verbal noun – have found themselves assimilated into current usage. In referring to electronic communication, *é-mail* too, in spite of its contested status, remains prevalent alongside *mél* (which, as the facts of use confirm, also ranges well outside its formally permitted role as an abbreviation).

Likewise, the long-proscribed *cocktail* exists in a range of constructions (*cocktail explosive*: 'explosive cocktail'; *bar à cocktail*: 'cocktail bar'; *cuiller à cocktail*: 'swizzle stick'; *robe à cocktail*: 'cocktail dress' ...). Irrespective of their proscription, feminizations too continue to gain currency; *sénetrice* is recorded alongside *senator*; *ingénieure*, (female) engineer, alongside *ingénieur*. The authority (and effects) of prescription in English were, as we might expect, no more secure. In spite of the 'barbarity' with which *lesser* was convicted in 1755, its citizenship in English has continued without obvious impediment.

As for Jerome, issues of authority, language, and dictionaries seem in fact to point in two very different directions. In the kind of governance which the rulings of academies (and academy dictionaries) embody, we can see that, rather than language driving the dictionary, it can conversely be the very existence of particular forms – *Internet, cocktail, computer* – which acts as a stimulus for both prescription (the recommendation for what should be used) and proscription (the recommendation for what should not). Taking a different perspective, however, it is also clear that the real processes of legitimization and citizenship, whether of words or meaning, instead take place in usage (and evidence of this). Power here comes from the masses. It is authority of this kind, based in the pull of language practice by the collective of users – the reality, in other words, of what people actually do in using a given language – which serves to explain the dominance of some loanwords (*le weekend, l'é-mail, le spam*) against the loss of others. Even if official documents can perhaps be made to toe the official line, policing everyday acts of usage is much more difficult.

Democracy and dictatorship

If language is a nation state, therefore, it is one which, in reality, recurrently affirms the truth of democracy rather than dictatorship, especially the kind of dictatorship which an individual lexicographer or group of lexicographers might seek to impose. History – and the long view of language change and development – again offers particularly timely lessons in this respect. If modern French (and indeed modern German) can express concern about the influx of non-native, and especially English, words, it can again be illuminating to glance at Johnson's work in the 18th century, a period in which it had been the excessive borrowing of words from French into English which provoked concerns about linguistic corruption and contamination. Unless checked, as Johnson warned, the British would, in the end, surely simply 'babble a dialect of *France*'.

Here too, the intended authority of the dictionary was brought into play. Entries such as *ruse* (declared to be 'A French word neither elegant nor necessary') or that for *manage* ('a phrase merely

Gallick; not to be imitated') served in Johnson's own dictionary as intentionally corrective measures, as did Johnson's determined silence on words such as *casserole, picturesque, reconnoitre,* or *clique* which, as contemporary writing confirms, were widely used in 18th-century English. Nevertheless, if we return to modern English, *ruse, manage* (together with Johnson's omitted French words) still, of course, remain. The authority of usage again prevails, irrespective of the concerns of either purism or 'correctness'.

Authority in terms of the power to control language is therefore not a strong point of what lexicographers do (or, indeed, what they aim to do when we consider modern descriptive lexicography). Nevertheless, narratives of legitimization can remain prevalent. 'Pre-texting, sub-prime, netroots accepted into Merriam-Webster lexicon' stated a headline in 2008 (*netroots,* formed on analogy with *grassroots,* is a new word, dated to 2003, which denotes political activists who communicate by means of the Internet, and especially by blogs). *The Times* one year later described the ways in which *twitter* had been 'accepted as a verb' in the new edition of *Collins English Dictionary.* Here too, however, the perceived currents of authority need to be reversed.

Views of this kind, for example, still construct dictionaries as gatekeepers (or border guards), selectively admitting words such as *twitter, sub-prime,* or *pre-text* ('to pretend to text someone or reply to a text message in order to avoid an awkward situation') on the basis that such words have, in some way, been judged worthy of being recorded. In contrast, the changing wordlists of descriptive dictionaries (and the new editions which are produced) simply reflect the diction of current use. The underlying premises are quantitative (based on the frequency and prevalence of particular forms) rather than qualitative (based on evaluations of 'good' or 'bad', legitimate or otherwise).

| Home | Concordance | Word List | Word Sketch | Thesaurus | Sketch-Diff |

| Turn on clustering | More data | Less data | Save |

sequentiality new_oec_plus_biwec_alt freq = 37

V obj N*	7	1.8
will	1	1.94
defy	1	0.2

X from-i N*	1	3.5
detachment	1	1.06

N* subj V	3	2.0
presuppose	1	2.92

X* in-i N	1	0.8
totalization	1	7.08

X mod N*	12	1.1
inexorable	1	3.61
spurious	1	2.66
perpetual	1	1.67
narrative	2	1.38
repetitive	1	1.09
relentless	1	1.03

and/or	8	1.8
periodicity	1	4.53
incongruity	1	4.05
incompatibility	1	2.45

X* into-i N	1	9.3
Now	1	0.55

X of-i N*	8	4.0
beginning-middle-end	1	11.42
exclusive	1	3.02

Authority

14. Screen shot of concordance for *sequentiality*, taken from the Oxford English Corpus

Paradoxically, it is language which, in this light, can be seen to dictate; the more a word or meaning is used, the greater is its right to inclusion in a dictionary. The descriptive dictionary-maker therefore simply records observable evidence as objectively as possible. Jerome's problems on *sequentiality* can be solved in the same way. Since *sequentiality* is used (by Jerome and others), it exists. Since, as Figure 14 illustrates, it is not a high-frequency item, not all dictionaries will necessarily record it.

If we return to the definitions of authority with which this chapter began, even if dictionary-users – and indeed, certain dictionary-makers – might endorse the view that the authority of the dictionary is indeed vested in 'the power to enforce laws, exact obedience, command, determine, or judge', close observation of language practice, as well as the kind of perspective which, as we have seen, is afforded by the long view of language change, reveals time and again that this is not so. Authority of this kind, as Johnson himself came to realize, is ultimately a chimera. 'Those who have been persuaded to think well of my design, require that it should fix our language, and put a stop to those alterations which time and chance have hitherto been suffered to make in it without opposition', he stated. If his dictionary enterprise had begun with aims of this kind, both time and experience enforced a valuable and judicious distance. 'With this consequence I will confess that I flattered myself for a while', Johnson instead confesses, 'but now begin to fear that I have indulged expectation which neither reason nor experience can justify'. Rather than valedictory triumph, it is the fallibility of aspiration – and the very real limits of what dictionaries are able to do – which emerge as the prime lesson to be learned.

Authority and authoritativeness

The real measure of authority for a dictionary instead resides in a rather different quality – that of being *authoritative* or, as the relevant definition in the *Bloomsbury English Dictionary* affirms, that of being 'reliable, backed by evidence, and showing deep knowledge'. As the American linguist Charles Fries declared in 1962, a dictionary can in fact be an authority 'only in the sense in which a book of chemistry or of physics or of botany can be an "authority" – by the accuracy and the completeness of its record of the observed facts of the field examined, in accord with the latest principles and techniques of the particular science'. It is this which links the dictionary securely to the second sense of authority in the *American Heritage Dictionary*: the dictionary as reference book in its status as 'an accepted source of expert information and advice'.

Authoritativeness of this kind likewise underpins the entries of the modern descriptive dictionary which, as previous chapters have shown, rest firmly on the careful and systematic assessment of usage. To consult *ruse* or *lesser* in a modern dictionary is therefore to encounter a simple statement of fact ('A clever stratagem or plan intended to deceive or trick'; 'Smaller; inferior; minor', the respective definitions in *Chambers Concise Dictionary* state). Information on spelling is similar, based on evidence rather than opinion. The dictionary as reference book sorts out with ease the unintentional influence of homophones (as in the inadvertent use of *baited breath* rather than *bated breath*, of *flare* when *flair* was intended, or the different semantic territories of *Viking hordes* and *Viking hoards*).

A number of fault-lines can nevertheless still be observed, dividing dictionary-users and dictionary-makers on the matter of authority and its proper location (and its limits). As Chapter 2 has explored, for example, it is, on one level, entirely true that the 19th century was witness to a revolution in the understanding of language – bringing a commitment to the objective, evidence-based approach that characterizes the modern descriptive dictionary text. Equally true, however, is the fact that it was a revolution that not everyone shared, and that many actively resisted. 'A dictionary is not a drag-net to bring up for us the broken pots and dead kittens, the sewerage of speech, as well as its living fishes', the American poet James Russell Lowell forcefully opined in the *Atlantic Monthly* in 1860: 'a lexicographer who rakes the books of second- and third-rate men for out-of-the-way phrases is doing us no favor'. As here, democratic inclusivity could seem like undiscerning liberalism. The verbal equivalents of broken pots (and dead kittens), Lowell argued, should be judged as such, and firmly cast aside.

Conflict and consensus

The treatments of labels, etymology, and sources all emerge as potentially controversial areas in this respect. In each, the nature of authority (and the kind of authority the dictionary can and should present) can be contested, revealing the influence of very different assumptions on the part of dictionary-makers and dictionary-users. Etymology, for instance, as its own etymology reveals, is the study of the 'true' or 'original' meaning of a word or form: *Etymologie*, 'true expounding', as Cawdrey's *Table Alphabeticall* early explained. It is as the result of etymological investigation that we know that, say, *tragedy* derives from the Greek for 'goat-song', or *juggernaut* from Hindi *Jagannāth* < Sanskrit *Jagannātha*, meaning 'lord of the world'. In historical lexicography, such as that of the *OED* or the Grimms' work in Germany, etymology is a starting point. Entries, here precisely like biographies, track changing meanings through time, from birth to – where relevant – obsolescence and death.

Etymology can, however, also provoke more partisan – and indeed prescriptive – responses. If one meaning is 'true', other meanings, especially those that emerge as part of later processes of change, could, for instance, equally be assumed to be false, not least since language change, as we have seen on a number of occasions, may popularly be regarded as evidence of decline. We can early see attitudes of this kind at work in the entry for *epigram* in John Bullokar's *English Expositor* of 1616. Here, the authority of the past in which, as Bullokar noted, *epigram* 'properly signifieth a superscription or writing set vpon any thing', is placed against newer meanings in which *epigram* 'is commonly taken for a short wittie poeme'. Current usage is set against etymological propriety.

Similar oppositions are easily detected in Johnson's work. If, as he admits, the 'more frequent' meaning of *trivial* is 'light; trifling; unimportant; inconsiderable', this is also 'less just' (or, he argues, both less accurate and less valid). The etymological authority of the meaning 'vile; worthless; vulgar; such as may be picked up in the highway' (which precisely reflects its Latinate derivation in *trivialis* < 'that may be found everywhere, common, commonplace, vulgar, ordinary') is, in his opinion, to be preferred.

History and usage, of course, present somewhat different evidence in this respect. Similar tensions – between past and present authority, between etymology and current usage – nevertheless underpin a number of ongoing conflicts about the kind of 'proper' meanings which dictionaries should provide. Words such as *alternative* or *media* provide useful test cases in this context. Deriving from Latin *alter* ('one of two'), *alternative* etymologically refers to two items alone. 'In strictness the word cannot be applied to more than *two* things', Charles Annandale firmly stated in 1881 in his authoritatively titled *Imperial Dictionary*. 'I had always understood that the word "alternative" is derived directly from the Latin *alter* – the other one of two', a recent letter to *The Times* contended; one can have 'several choices, options, possibilities' – but not several alternatives, the writer added, once again firmly aligning etymology and correctness.

Language practice, on the other hand, is rather different. William Gladstone, Prime Minister of Britain when Annandale crafted his dictionary, referred to four alternatives, as the *OED* confirms ('My decided preference is for the fourth and last of these alternatives'). An even earlier example was located by the *OED* in John Stuart Mill's *Political Economy* (1846): 'The alternative seemed to be either death, or to be permanently supported by other people, or a radical change in the economical arrangements'. As here, etymology can point one way, and evidence of usage (even by highly educated writers) in another – in ways which are not necessarily reconcilable. Images of authority in turn divide between what is known as the *etymological fallacy* (in which the *etymon* – the 'original' or 'true' meaning of a word – must remain its meaning) and the kind of evidence which instead derives from empirical engagement with the facts of usage, and the rather different meanings these can present.

Modern dictionaries nevertheless engage with the absence of consensus in this and other words with marked clarity. 'Some traditionalists maintain, from an etymological standpoint, that you can only have two alternatives', the *New Oxford American Dictionary* (*NOAD*) hence noted under *alternative* in 2005. Attitudes and evidence were nevertheless sharply distinguished. 'Such uses are, however, normal in modern standard English', *NOAD* instead affirmed. As its evidence proved, *alternative* was – and is – widely used in structures in which reference is made to two, three, or more items. 'True meaning' was firmly placed in current use, irrespective of the etymological history of a word.

NOAD's Introduction presents a particularly clear statement of its position on such matters. 'The usage notes in the *New Oxford American Dictionary* take the view that English is English, not Latin, and that English is, like all living languages, subject to change', it states. In this light, 'good usage is usage that gets the speaker's or writer's message across, not usage that conforms to some arbitrary rules that fly in the face of historical fact or current evidence'. The 'good dictionary' is defined in the same way: 'a good dictionary reports the language as it is, not as the editors (or anyone else) would wish it to be, and the usage notes must give guidance that accords with observed facts about present-day usage'. For the modern lexicographer, the fact that *media* derives etymologically from the Latin plural of *medium* (and was therefore traditionally plural in itself) is of far less import than is the accurate documentation of current patterns of use. Or as the relevant entry in *NOAD* confirms:

> In practice, in the sense 'television, radio, the press, and the internet, collectively', **media** behaves as a collective noun (like *staff* or *clergy*, for example), which means that it is now acceptable in standard English for it to take either a singular or a plural verb.

Usage notes of the kind discussed above – balanced, reasoned, and securely objective – clearly also participate in the changed image of authority which characterizes the modern descriptive dictionary. Earlier dictionary-makers, for instance, often strove to constrain particular forms of usage using a strikingly authoritarian – and densely evaluative – diction. Disfavoured words and meanings could be convicted of being 'vulgar' or 'ludicrous', 'sloppy' or 'incorrect', 'improper' or 'low', or plain 'wrong'. The construction *to have rather* was 'barbarous', Johnson stated under *rather* (*will rather* was better, he thought). Notions of acceptability can provoke strikingly forthright opinion. '*Raise* should never be used of bringing human beings to maturity; it is a misuse common in the southern and western United States. Cattle are *raised*; human beings are *brought up*', as *Funk & Wagnalls New Standard Dictionary*, edited by Frank Vizetelly, stated in 1913.

Such patterns, however, simply return us once more to the conflicted nature of the dictionary as nation state – and the legitimacy of dictatorship or democracy within it. Authority becomes a fraught territory in which prescriptive correctness and descriptive usage can seem permanently at odds. The usage information provided by modern dictionaries nevertheless often usefully engages with ongoing areas of variation and change. While change is given its due, so too are patterns of usage where language attitudes might make a degree of caution necessary, particularly in formal spheres of use. This too can be a part of the descriptive remit of modern lexicography.

Ongoing change in the meaning of *fortuitous* – and how this is treated in modern dictionaries – provides further illustration here. On one side, its etymology supports the sense 'that which happens or is produced by fortune or chance; accidental' (deriving ultimately from Latin *forte* 'by chance', *fors* 'chance'). On the other stands the newer transferred sense, 'happening by a lucky chance; fortunate' (as in 'It was really fortuitous that I met him today'). As the *New Zealand Oxford Dictionary* signals in its own choice of labels for this entry, this new sense can indeed be 'disputed'. 'Disputed', as the front-matter of the dictionary explains, here deftly 'indicates a use that is ... often regarded as erroneous or controversial'. Meanwhile, the decision to include the label 'colloquial' within the new sense itself serves instead to confirm its statistical prevalence in informal use.

The entry for *hopefully* (in the sense 'it is to be hoped') prompts similar guidance, flagging language attitudes ('it is still considered incorrect by some people') alongside the facts of language in use (this sense remains 'extremely common'). Value judgements are not endorsed. Instead, their existence is simply made part of the wider explanatory information about words and usage with which the dictionary-user is provided. Neutrality remains the dominant mode. Where conflicts about usage arise, the aim is, in essence, to be as objective as possible both about language use and about the subjectivities that attitudes and opposition can reflect.

Contesting the authority of evidence

The nature of the sources used as evidence can present other aspects of contested authority. Dictionary-making, as we have seen in Chapter 3, early inclined to hierarchical models of evidence in which the 'best' writers were deemed to provide examples of the 'best' language. Such examples were seen not only as illustrating words in use but as exemplifying them, even if, in so doing, they could provide a reference model that was remote from the realities of ordinary use. The expanding range of sources and source types used as dictionaries sought to become more representative could nevertheless provoke outright concern. Early responses to the first edition of the *OED*, for example, could reveal marked anxiety about what appeared to be its undue liberalism on matters of evidence. As *The Times* contended in 1884, even if the *OED* was clearly (and intentionally) 'by no means della Cruscan in its selection of words', surely a 'classical standard of writing' should be maintained in selecting evidence. A word such as *acrobatically* – included in the very first part of the dictionary – was, as another reviewer commented, verified 'by the somewhat questionable authority' of Rhoda Broughton, a prolific and popular writer of sensation fiction. Citations from canonical writers such as Dickens or Tennyson meanwhile passed unremarked.

Popular opinion on sources and the divergent authority they might possess, of course, returns us to the kinds of questions about identity – and mistaken identity – and the dictionary which have already been discussed in Chapter 1. Does the dictionary exist as a record of the language that is used, or of the 'best' language? Does it tell us what *is* used, or advise us on what *should* be used, providing not just examples but exemplary modes to be adopted? Is 'real' authority descriptive or prescriptive?

The enduring nature of these tensions, however, perhaps surfaces with most clarity not in the debates that surrounded the *OED* but in the critical response that greeted the publication in America of *Webster's Third International Dictionary*. Edited by Philip Gove and published in 1961, *Webster's Third* in some ways, of course, simply built on the precedents already established by the earlier Webster dictionaries. *Webster's New International Dictionary* of 1934, for example, had proudly vaunted its own empirical status as a 'Citation Dictionary' in which 'all the definitions are based on citations'. Authority and evidence worked together, establishing the foundations on which secure lexicographic analysis was to be built.

The citation file for *Webster's Third* was expanded to contain almost 4,500,000 new quotations (millions more had been consulted in other secondary sources such as the *OED*, or the four-volume *Dictionary of American English on Historical Principles* (1938–44) edited by William Craigie). For Gove, this new haul of evidence was to be used to document the idiomatic texture of contemporary 20th-century usage. New entries for words such as *litter bug*, *blast-off*, and *no-show* ('a person who reserves space on a train, a ship, or esp. an airplane but who neither uses nor cancels the reservation') were crafted. An elegantly precise definition accompanied the entry for *beatnik*: 'a person having a predilection for unconventional behavior and dress and often a preoccupation with exotic philosophizing and self-expression'. A deliberate engagement with recent evidence, including that of reported speech, characterized the selection of citations; *goof* ('a blunder or mistake') was supported by a citation from Dwight Eisenhower; *sick* by one from Elizabeth Taylor ('a room smelling rather of sick'). 'Two shows a day drain a girl', as Ethel Merman stated under *drain* in a citation which attracted particular censure. Merman also supported *goof* as a verb ('somebody had goofed'). While major writers such as Hawthorne still appear ('snatching with ghostly hands at scepters', as a quotation under *ghostly* affirms), evidence could smack of the colloquial and informal, the ordinary rather than extraordinary – tracking, just as Gove intended, typical American usage of the mid-20th century.

Labelling strategies changed too. *Ain't* in *Webster's New International* of 1934 had been characterized as dialectal and 'illiterate'. It was now simply accompanied by the statement that it was 'used orally in most parts of the U.S. by many cultivated speakers' (even if, as Gove also added, it was 'disapproved of by many'). Authority was firmly located in real language, and the testimony this was seen to offer. 'A dictionary', as Gove's preface resolutely affirmed, should 'state meanings in which words are in fact used, not … give editorial opinion on what these meanings should be'.

A conspicuous absence of neutrality conversely hallmarked many reviews. 'The dictionary's traditional function was to establish normal usage, which means norms', the *National Review* expostulated, giving little credence to the idea of descriptive rather than prescriptive processes. 'This abdication of responsibility for the standards of language is deplorable', a review (headed 'Logomachy – Debased Verbal Currency') in the *American Bar Association Journal* likewise declared, castigating the ways in which the dictionary had apparently 'utterly abdicated any role as judge of what is good English usage'.

Webster's Third was, in this light, seen as representative in the wrong ways. If the 'good' dictionary should prescribe (and proscribe), Gove's work was, of course, seriously awry. Forms such as the contested verb *to finalize* ('to put in final or finished form') were recorded in line with the democratic realities of usage, rather than the assumed niceties of 'good' American English. 'Soon my conclusions will be finalized', a quotation from Eisenhower stated. The satirical writer S. J. Perelman added further testimony ('the couple finalized plans to marry at once'). Similar was the primary sense of *nauseous*, which was now specified as 'affected with or inclined to nausea'. The traditional meaning 'causing or such as might be inclined to cause nausea' was relegated into second place, again to the disgust of conservatively minded critics. Gove refused to dictate. 'If a word is used often enough, it becomes a fact of usage', he argued. Usage – and evidence of this – justified the ways in which *nauseous* had been treated in the dictionary. Entries that attracted controversy – such as that for *don't* (used as a contraction for 'does not', as in 'she don't believe in ghosts') – were, he likewise insisted, 'a carefully accurate report of the facts'. As contemporary evidence on both usage and language attitudes proved, *don't* was indeed 'often used with a singular subject by cultivated speakers', even though, by precisely the same token, 'the construction is sometimes objected to'.

Gove's own definition of the good dictionary remained, as we might expect, rather different. Dictionary-making, he noted, 'should have no traffic with guesswork, prejudice, or bias or with artificial notions of correctness and superiority'. It was instead embedded in a representativeness which was itself based in the facts rather than the fictions of use. 'It must be descriptive not prescriptive', he affirmed. Only if founded on principles of this kind could a dictionary legitimately act as an accurate indicator of how language is used. 'If a dictionary should neglect the obligation to act as a faithful recorder and interpreter of usage, no matter what revisions may be called for, it cannot expect to be any longer appealed to as an authority.'

The authority of the dictionary is therefore not necessarily where we might expect it to lie. As in the metaphors of nature which Johnson came to deploy, in which change is a process of both 'budding and falling away', a living language cannot in reality be either fixed or rendered static. The authority of a dictionary is powerless in such contexts; no dictionary, as Johnson eloquently noted, can be an elixir, proffering timelessness in the face of the currents of ongoing change. That *attachment* is now used most frequently in the sense 'a file that is sent as an email' (rather than 'The fact or condition of being attached by love or devotion') is a fact of current English, not evidence of decline. Similar is *miniscule* in the sense 'very small', a usage labelled as 'erroneous' throughout the 20th century (the correct form was deemed to be *minuscule*). In a revised entry on *OED Online*, dated to March 2010, both form and sense now appear without comment; accompanying evidence dates back to 1909. Authoritativeness, as here, lies in the capacity to engage with current evidence and to adjust entries and senses accordingly based on a careful and objective interpretation of the facts.

This does not, on the other hand, mean that all changes or variants are immediately recorded (or indeed recorded at all). A judicious conservatism can be sensible; after all, not all changes are adopted. At what point variation (and the emergence of new senses) is described remains a problematic issue. Even reputable writers can make mistakes. Both George Eliot and Elizabeth Gaskell, for instance, used *euphuism* when both clearly meant *euphemism* (' "If anything did – go wrong, you know", said Cynthia, using an euphuism for death', as Gaskell wrote in her novel *Wives and Daughters* in 1865; 'Those are your roundabout euphuisms that dress up swindling', Eliot stated one year later in *Felix Holt, the Radical*).

Sarah Palin's recent use of *refudiate* (an interesting blend of *refute* 'to disprove or deny' and *repudiate* 'to refuse or cease to acknowledge') also comes under this heading. *Militate* and *mitigate* ('to make less harsh or hostile') are 'sometimes confused', *NOAD* warns, for instance, in a usage note under *militate* ('to have influence or effect'). Even if used by the novelist William Faulkner ('some intangible and invisible social force that mitigates against him'), this is still a 'mistake', Merriam-Webster likewise avers. *Flaunt* ('to display ostentatiously') and *flout* ('to treat with a kind of contemptuous disregard') can elicit similar cautions. 'A word sometimes confused with [*flaunt*] is *flout*', states *Chambers Concise Dictionary*; '*flaunt* is still sometimes wrongly used where *flout* is meant: they must be prevented from *flouting* not *flaunting* the law', *Collins English Dictionary* confirms.

The same shift is, however, widely taken as evidence of a change in progress by contemporary linguists. As this suggests, the reference models provided by dictionaries can, as here, tend to err on the safe side. Ultimately, however, once a change has diffused through the language community, it must be recorded neutrally and in its own right, irrespective of the language attitudes of the lexicographer, who may or may not share the change in question. 'A reliable dictionary', as Atkins and Rundell emphasize, 'is one whose generalisations about word behaviour approximate closely to the ways in which people normally see (and understand) language when engaged in real communicative acts (such as writing novels or business reports, reading newspapers, or having conversations)'. Only authority (and authoritativeness) of this kind can offer accurate – and truthful – information to language-users who turn to a dictionary in search of illumination and advice.

Chapter 5
Truth

That dictionaries engage with truth is a commonplace in the history of lexicography. The 'table alphabetical' which Edmund Coote inserted in his *English Schoole-maister* of 1596 was, he stated, intended to teach 'true writing', as well as the 'understanding of any hard, English word'. 'True meaning' is given prominence in John Cowell's 1607 *Interpreter*, a dictionary of law and legal terms, just as it is by, say, Samuel Johnson, Jr – an American lexicographer who in fact pre-dates Webster by some years; Johnson's *School Dictionary* of 1798 promised 'true meaning and pronunciation of the most useful words in the ENGLISH LANGUAGE'. Truth, seen in terms of the facts rather than the fictions of usage, was, as we have seen in the previous chapter, likewise integral to Philip Gove's conception of the good dictionary – however unpalatable such truths may at times have seemed to the early reviewers of *Webster's Third*.

Truth can, however, remain strikingly difficult to achieve. Factual errors, as we have seen in Johnson's entry for *pastern* (discussed in Chapter 1), can all too easily intervene. The French scientist Georges Cuvier's response to the 'immortels' of the Académie Française on the subject of their proposed definition of *crab* ('a little red fish that walks backwards') presents another famous example of lexicographical untruth: 'Admirable, gentlemen', as Cuvier is reputed to have said: 'most satisfactory: at the same time to be hypercritical, I may take leave to point out three trifling faults in it. A crab is not a little fish; it is not red, and it does not walk backwards: but with these small exceptions, the definition is perfect.' *Howitzer* in the *OED* similarly went awry. Defined as 'a short piece of ordnance ... specially designed for the horizontal firing of shells with small charges', the 'true meaning', as Murray was informed after publication, was precisely the opposite. 'I don't know who can have given you the definition of "Howitzer"', a letter from Major John Leslie in November 1913 states: 'Horizontal is the exact contrary. It is essentially a high-angle firing weapon, and would never, under any circumstances, be fired horizontally.'

Here problems of truthfulness – and untruth – can be revealed in relatively objective ways. Other entries, however, are far more complex, revealing the ways in which definitions (and the truths they are assumed to convey) can be aligned along the fault-lines of belief and behaviour, of moral or political authority, or of bias and prejudice. John Cowell's definitions of words such as *king*, *parliament*, and *prerogative* (stating that parliament did not have authority over an absolute monarchy) were, for example, viewed as approaching lexicographical – and political – heresy rather than the 'true meaning' his title page had promised. The *Interpreter* was not only banned (with extant copies recalled by the mayor of London) but was burned by the public hangman on 26 March 1610. Cowell himself resigned from the Chair of Civil Law at Cambridge which he had hitherto occupied, and was imprisoned. Truth here was divided; Cowell's truth did not accord with the truths preferred by the government (which insisted on its own authority in this respect). Definition – the wrong 'truth' – can render lexicography a surprisingly dangerous profession.

Even when the observable facts seem to be in agreement, interpretation can differ. Is, for example, a *potato* 'one of the greatest blessings bestowed on man by the Creator', as defined by Noah Webster in his *American Dictionary of the English Language* – or simply 'a starchy vegetable that grows underground' (the definition preferred by *Collins English Dictionary*)? Similarly, is *prostitution* 'The offering of the body to indiscriminate lewdness', as the relevant entry stated in the first edition of the *OED*, or is it, as the *Bloomsbury English Dictionary* affirms, here in a rather different tone, 'the act of engaging in sexual intercourse ... in exchange for money'? Are *gypsies* 'a race of vagabonds who infest Europe, Africa, and Asia, strolling about and subsisting mostly by theft, robbery, and fortune-telling' (as Chauncey Goodrich declared in his 1856 edition of Webster's *Dictionary*); 'a wandering race known in Western Europe from 1417 ... dark-skinned, dark-eyed, lithe, and sinewy ... living largely in tents, huts, or caves, and are generally fortune-tellers, musicians, cattle-dealers, or tinkers' (as in Isaac Funk's *Standard Dictionary* of 1893); or, to return once more to the *Bloomsbury English Dictionary*, is *gypsy* in fact 'an offensive term for a member of the Roma people'?

As Ephraim Chambers pertinently observed in his *Cyclopedia* of 1728, 'if we can't deduce the Nature of a Dictionary from the Condition of the Author; we may the Conditions of the Author from the Nature of a Dictionary'. As this chapter will explore, dictionaries can in fact engage with truth, and perceived truths, from a variety of perspectives. Indeed, rather than acting as embodiments of neutrality and truth-telling, as in their conventionally assumed role, dictionaries can instead emerge as all too human products, reflecting and refracting dominant assumptions about gender, race, and nation as well as displaying a didacticism which readily extends to questions – and evaluations – of morality and faith.

Nations and national mutabilities: retelling the truth

Ideas of language and nationhood can be particularly productive in this context. 'A national language is a national tie', Noah Webster early affirmed, stressing the need for new truths in post-revolution America: 'As an independent nation, our honor requires us to have a system of our own, in language as well as government.' This principle of linguistic independence would, for Webster, involve careful consideration of what American English should contain – and what it should, in turn, reject.

The stratified (and eminently British) language of *rank* was a case in point. The popularity of 18th-century dictionaries such as William Perry's *Royal Standard Dictionary* or John Walker's *Critical Pronouncing Dictionary and Expositor of the English Language* (as well, of course, as Johnson's own work) was, for instance, seen as especially problematic. Such dictionaries were widely used in America, embodying, for Webster, versions of truth which were surely remote from a 'free people' inspired by the 'noble sentiments of liberty and patriotism'.

Lexicography here is seen as a way of imaging both nation and identity, dividing the old and new world, as well as carefully repositioning relevant truths. *Rank*, for instance, was defined by Johnson in an extensive entry which details meanings such as 'range of subordination' and 'class, order', as well as 'dignity, high place, as in *he is a man of rank*'. Webster determinedly excluded it. 'In the *United States* … titles and distinctions of rank do not exist', Webster's entry for *gentleman* proclaims. The language (and assumptions) of social hierarchy which Johnson's dictionary affirms are instead distanced both geographically and politically. *Gentleman* in the sense 'the servant of a man of rank, who attends his person' is given as specific to 'Great Britain'. In America, in contrast, *gentleman* is 'to be applied to every man of education and of good breeding' (a meaning that, as Webster adds with approval, is also emerging in popular use in Britain).

Entries for *democrat* and *democratical* offer other examples of the ways in which different images of truth can be fostered or repelled. *Democrat* (absent from Johnson's dictionary) assumes new and central significance in Webster's work: 'One who adheres to a government by the people, or favors the extension of the right of suffrage to all classes of men'. Johnson's citations for *democratical* (which he did include) orientated meaning in rather different – and distinctly negative – directions ('They are still within the line of vulgarity, and are *democratical* enemies to truth'; 'As the Government of England has a mixture of *democratical* in it, so the right of inventing political lyes, is partly in the people').

As in equally telling entries for words such as *congress* or *president*, or *independence*, what is 'true' in Britain can thereby be rendered no longer 'true' in America (and, of course, vice-versa). *Monarchy* is equally illuminating; defined using Britain as an example ('the same name is sometimes given to a kingdom or state in which the power of the king or supreme magistrate is limited by a constitution, or by fundamental laws. Such is the British monarchy. Hence we speak of absolute or despotic monarchies, and of limited monarchies'), Webster meanwhile moves on to draw a different truth: 'A free government has a great advantage over a simple monarchy'.

Webster's *American Dictionary*, like his other works on language, can therefore offer a deft repositioning of meaning, language, and nation in ways that are precisely in line with his wider views on education (and the role of educational texts such as dictionaries) in shaping the distinctive identity of nationhood in the new world. Conversely, such aims can, of course, be resisted – and other truths intentionally reclaimed. 'The very title of Dr. Webster's Dictionary indicates a radical misapprehension as to the nature and office of such a work. He calls the result of his labors an "American Dictionary of the English Language," as if provincialism were a merit', as an anonymous reviewer in the *Atlantic Monthly* forcefully contended in 1860. American English here was not a language, but a dialect – 'provincial' in its distance from British English. Further ideological weight was added to the writer's views on nations (and lexicographical legitimization) by an intentionally illuminating analogy. 'Fancy a "Cuban Dictionary of the Spanish Language"', he exclaimed: 'It would be of value only to the comparative philologist, curious in the changes of meaning, pronunciation, and the like, which circumstances are always bringing about in languages subjected to new conditions of life and climate.'

Other configurations of power and nation (as well as the deliberate fostering of particular models of truth at the expense of others) can easily be seen at work in, say, the missionary dictionaries which proliferated over the 19th century, as in works such as *An Anglo-Burmese Dictionary* 'Published for the Use of Schools' by Reverend G. H. Hough, or the *Kaffir-English Dictionary* written by the Reverend Albert Kropf, Superintendent of the Berlin Mission, South Africa, in 1899. The linguistic aims of such missionary dictionaries may indeed have been laudable, recording as they did a range of hitherto unresearched language varieties. Nevertheless, a sense of cultural normativity (and embedded cultural hierarchy) is often all too evident. Hough's work, for example, was directed at what he described as the language of 'an ignorant and semi-barbarian people', for whom English could provide not only education but civilization too.

A similar perspective is evident in the *Tahitian and English Dictionary, with Introductory Remarks on the Polynesian Language* (1851) by John Davies. The 'introductory remarks' that he provides explicitly engage with 'the Language of a rude and uncivilized people' which 'has, as might be expected, many deficiencies, when compared with the highly cultivated and polished languages of Europe'. If Polynesian is allowed to possess a certain 'force' and 'simplicity', this simply reveals other patterns of cultural stereotyping at work. Truth, seen in this light, can be dangerously partisan.

As Derek Peterson has argued, missionary dictionaries can, as a result, often be seen as 'functional tools of colonial power'; a way, in effect, of colonizing language as well as territory, and of imposing particular structures of meaning by means of a dominantly colonial gaze.

Modern dictionary-making, documenting endangered languages such as Navajo or Sora (a language in Eastern India), tends to work from very different ideological principles.

Imperial truths

The status of the dictionary as a 'historical monument' which reflects 'history seen from one point of view' – an image used by Richard Trench in his 1857 lectures to the Philological Society – can therefore be striking. Trench's words, of course, form part of a detailed exploration of the kind of lexicographical practice which established the guiding – and eminently historical – principles of the *OED*. They also, however, suggest something of the ideological consequences which such a historical point of view can also comport. If history is, on the one hand, objectively documented through a mass of dated evidence, it is also constructed and narrated, as well as filtered through particular patterns of selection and interpretation. 'How can there be a true History, when we see no man living is able to write truly the History of the last week?', as Sir Will demands in Thomas Shadwell's play *The Squire of Alsatia* (1688) in a quotation which appears in the *OED*'s own entry for *history*. Other accompanying quotations (such as Thomas Carlyle's view of history as a 'distillation of Rumour', or Macaulay's image of 'The huge Mississippi of falsehood called history') likewise suggest that even history is not always what it seems.

The ways in which the first edition of the *OED* is embedded in particular images of Victorian history – and engaged in relating distinctly colonial narratives – are especially interesting in this context. James Murray's images of what he termed 'Anglicity' in the lectures he himself gave to the Philological Society in 1880 and 1881 certainly correlate closely with the kind of colonial diction evident, as we have seen, in Davies's work on Polynesian. Discourses of civilization (and its antonyms) frame Murray's definition of English as 'the language of a civilized nation', 'a great, cultivated, civilized language'. English is, in turn, described as firmly 'distinct from the scanty idiom of a barbarous tribe'.

That similar patterns of cultural hierarchy – and cultural normativity – can be detected in the dictionary itself is therefore perhaps unsurprising. *Canoe* in the first edition of the *OED* is, for example, explicitly equipped with both 'civilized' and 'uncivilized' senses. For the latter, a *canoe* is 'a kind of boat in use among uncivilized nations' where it is 'used generally for any rude craft in which uncivilized people go upon the water'. 'Most savages use paddles instead of oars', as Murray decided to add in the interests of further elucidation. Sense 2 of *canoe* instead offered a meaning 'in civilized use'. Here, the evaluative diction of rudeness and savagery disappears; a *canoe* is simply 'a small light sort of boat or skiff propelled by paddling'.

A similar divide informed Murray's chosen definition of *blanket*. If its core meaning is 'chiefly ... one of the principal covering of a bed', we are also told that blankets have another role, as when they are 'used by savages and destitute persons, for clothing'. Close scrutiny of the way in which different meanings are presented serves, however, to reveal the ideological positions that are at stake. A significant difference, for instance, clearly lurks in the gap between the declarative statement that a *blanket* is, by definition, 'the principal covering of a bed' (especially when *bed* has already been defined as 'a regular item of household furniture in civilized life') – and the information that a blanket is merely 'used ... for' clothing. The phrasing of dictionary entries is rarely accidental; 'used ... for', as a turn of phrase, deftly suggests divergence from its 'true' role (and especially when compounded by use of the culturally loaded 'savages' within the same definition).

Similar images of otherness and cultural deficit are widely perceptible, revealing the ways in which, for dictionaries, definition (and notions of truth) can be bound by notions of culture and class, and of 'us' and 'them'. 'A cloth; the piece of cloth forming originally the single item of clothing variously worn by the natives of hot countries: … by uncivilized races', the first edition of the *OED* stated for *pagne*.

The diction of civilization and its antonyms can be pervasive. *Pottage* provides a similar example; 'no longer a term of English cookery', this can, we are told, still be used to refer to 'the soups of savage peoples'. While some words and meanings are 'civilized', intimations of 'savagery' act as distancing devices (*fetishes*: 'An inanimate object worshipped by savages on account of its supposed magical powers'; *dirt-eating*: 'The eating of some kinds of clay or earth as food, practiced by some savage tribes'; *war-dances*: 'a dance performed by a savage tribe before a warlike excursion'). In the first edition of the *OED*, such forms are both made English, by being incorporated within the dictionary (and attested within works by English writers) – but also rendered profoundly un-English by the nature of their definitions and the all too negative connotations that these are made to contain. Modern dictionaries offer swift ideological correctives – *war-dance*: 'a dance that members of some tribes traditionally performed before or after a battle', notes *Encarta*; *pottage* is simply 'a thick vegetable, or meat and vegetable, soup'.

Cultural scripts and the dictionary

As such examples confirm, dictionaries are bound to time and place in ways that repeatedly remind us of the surprising mutability of 'truth', and of the radical changes that can intervene in what might be deemed a 'good' (or indeed a 'bad') definition. For the readers of the original *OED*, the widespread diction of savagery and civilization went unremarked. Instead, ethnocentricity – the positioning of 'truth' in terms of preferential readings of language, nation, and cultural norms – merely confirmed, from the point of view of history, the making of the dictionary within a strikingly imperial century in which the colonies act as a frequent reference point, and the colonial gaze is, as we have seen, often all too perceptible.

That Murray and his co-editors were not alone in such cultural scripts is, of course, also clear. 'One of a race of the human species belonging to that division of mankind which is characterised by the possession of hair of a woolly or crisp nature', stated Charles Annandale under *negro* in his 1881 edition of the *Imperial Dictionary*:

> Negroes are not only distinguished from the other races by their black colour, but also by various other peculiarities; such as the projection of the whole visage in advance of the forehead; the prolongation of the upper and lower jaws; the small facial angle; the flatness of the forehead and of the hinder part of the head; the short broad, and flat nose and the thick protruding lips, as well as by the woolly hair mentioned.

That such legacies also long continued in lexicography is a fact equally in evidence. The American lexicographer J. R. R. Hulbert, discussing the best way to define *negro* in 1955, positions an ideal of lexicographical truth in ways that would now be seen as highly problematic. To define *negro* as 'An individual of the Negro race' was, he argued, entirely inadequate: 'What is required is something like this: "A member of a black or black-brown race, found originally in Africa, notable for thick lips, kinky hair", etc.'

The lexicographical practice of half a century later instead presents us with very different readings, ones in which the discriminatory diction of otherness is absent and a conspicuous equality of presentation instead takes centre stage. Such strategies of revision (and the publication of new and modernized editions) confirm, however, the ways in which the perceived truths of one period can, in turn, be rephrased and renegotiated, in line with other images of history and legitimate truth, in another. As in the strategically rewritten versions of *pagne* in different editions of the *OED*, patterns of retelling enact their own cultural – and deliberately different – histories. In the second edition of the *OED*, published in 1989, a new uneasiness about the implications of 'civilized' means that it has deftly been replaced by 'Westernized'. The derogatory diction of the 'uncivilized' is silenced entirely. Still, great cultural revision is evident in the redrafted text of *OED Online*, dated September 2009. Here, the interpretative lens has been refocused, and African usage is made the centre of explanation and interest. Discriminatory diction is replaced by exemplary neutrality. In a similar way, 'savages' have now been elided from *blanket*, and the 'uncivilized' meanings of *canoe* likewise disappear from view. African lexicography, for a range of languages, meanwhile reclaims both words and meanings in other ways entirely.

Pagne OED2 1989

A cloth; the piece of cloth forming originally the single article of clothing variously worn by natives of hot countries; *spec.* a loin-cloth, or a short petticoat, worn by primitive peoples, or retained by the westernized as part of their costume.

pagne, n. OED Online DRAFT REVISION Sept. 2009

In West Africa: a length of cloth, *esp.* one worn draped around the waist or forming a tunic (now chiefly by women). Also: the material from which this is made.

New labels such as 'offensive' likewise make explicit the operation of very different cultural norms within modern lexicography. *Negro* (noun): 'an offensive term for a black person', states the *Bloomsbury English Dictionary. Darkey* ('a negro, a blacky'), Murray had conversely noted in 1893, offering the label 'colloquial'. 'A Black, esp. a Southern U.S. Black', *OED2* in 1989 instead averred, once more reconfiguring the boundaries of acceptable meaning in the light of both historical and cultural change. Even here, though, the choice of labelling might surprise ('usually considered patronizing or mildly offensive'). Perceptions of truth in the 21st century have now moved on yet again.

Similar revisions can attend *Palestinian*. '(Native or inhabitant) of Palestine; (person) seeking to displace Israelis from Palestine', stated a new entry for the latter in the sixth edition of the *Concise Oxford Dictionary*, published in 1976. The dictionary here became an eloquent image of disputed territory in both geographical and political terms. A revised definition was inserted after considerable controversy and complaint: 'Native or inhabitant of Palestine' and, used adjectivally, 'Of, pertaining to, or connected with, Palestine'. If this was seen as representing 'a victory for truth and objectivity' by the *Egyptian Gazette*, the response from certain Israeli and Jewish readers was, however, rather different. 'In describing a Palestinian as a native or inhabitant of Palestine, you implicitly deny the existence of the state of Israel', the editors of the *Concise* were informed. 'Truth' had been lost rather than gained – or gained rather than lost, depending on one's point of view.

Too much truth: taboo and the dictionary

The precise nature of truth (and the truths dictionaries can or should tell) can therefore be difficult to establish. Like other contested borders, what is deemed legitimate on one side may be viewed in different ways by others, even when endeavours are clearly being made to establish the facts of language. The nature of what can, or should, be recorded in dictionaries (and whether certain truths of both language and usage should be withheld altogether) can be particularly problematic here. Sex and sexuality – and truths of this kind – are a case in point. The question of what dictionaries should do in this domain has long posed problems; are the facts to be recorded, or a decorous silence maintained? Even if relevant headwords are included, thereby descriptively acknowledging their role in the 'inventory' of the language, what should the dictionary-maker do in terms of definition when a host of trangressions in terms of propriety might have to be committed?

For dictionary-makers in the past, such questions were resolved in a variety of ways. Latin, as we have seen, had long been established as the shared language of learning. It could, however, also assume a role as equally learned disguise, enabling dictionary-makers to include problematic words in English while defining them in ways which denied elucidation to those who did not have an extensive grounding in classical Latin. '*Foeminem subagitare*' ('to lie with a woman illicitly') stated Nathaniel Bailey under *fuck*, exploiting a strategic bilingualism in what was formally, of course, an entirely monolingual work. Even the Latin, however, maintained a coy indirection.

Latin as decorous disguise was to be the solution adopted for a range of words in the seven-volume *Slang and its Analogues* ('a dictionary historical and comparative of the heterodox speech of all classes of society for more than three hundred years') written by John Farmer and William Henley in the late 19th century. Given the nature of their dictionary (and its contents), Farmer and Henley inevitably had to confront a number of problems in this respect. Private letters, narrating behind the scenes dilemmas, again enable us to glimpse difficulties and decision-making at first hand. As Farmer acknowledged in a private letter to James Murray, decency and definition could, for the lexicographer, often seem irreconcilable. 'I have been casting about for devices for obscuring, as far as possible, any unpleasant words with which I have to deal', he wrote.

As Farmer's letter confirms, compromises in terms of decency could, however, lead to compromises in the very nature of what dictionaries normally strove to achieve. Paradoxically, the explanation of certain words had to be phrased in such a way as to deny elucidation for the mass of readers who might consult them. As Farmer explained to Murray, therefore, he had had to settle on a language 'not understanded of the people'. Latin was part of a conscious strategy, intentionally veiling undesirable meanings from ordinary readers, especially women and children. Meanwhile, those with classical erudition (who were clearly assumed to be able to cope with such indecorous content) could simply bypass such devices.

Euphemism, obfuscation, or simple silence all play similar roles in other works. Revisions instituted by the early American lexicographer Samuel Johnson, Jr in the second edition of his *School Dictionary* provide an interesting snapshot in this context. The first edition, published in 1789, was written independently. The second (enlarged) edition, published two years later, was a collaborative work, written with the Yale-educated Reverend John Elliott. 'Delicacy and chastity of language' emerges as a new area of concern in the 'true meaning' which is now promised. 'The indiscriminate use of vulgar or indecent words proliferates in contemporary dictionary-making', the preface argues: 'Many words there found are highly offensive to a modest ear and cannot be read without a blush'.

Given that the dictionary in question was one intended for educational use, some purging among the headwords that had been included in the first edition seems sensible (neither *bedswerver* 'one who is false to the bed' or *belswagger* 'a whore master', for example, seem suitable for the kind of rote-learning of the dictionary often practised by schoolchildren at this time). Delicacy would, however, also lead to some uneasy compromises in terms of definition, and the explanatory role a dictionary should play. *Faeces*, defined in 1798 as 'dregs, excrement', becomes the highly euphemistic 'dregs, settlings' in 1800; *seraglio*, 'a house for women of pleasure' in 1798, becomes simply 'a house for women', a rephrasing which thereby inadvertently suggests the potential use of *seraglio* in describing a convent or nunnery. Meaning becomes opaque, compromising the role of the dictionary in itself.

Images of cultural and linguistic taboo, whether for children or general readers, in fact prove widely problematic in lexicographical history. If we return to Farmer and Henley's *Slang and its Analogues*, for example, it is clear that their lexicographical caution was probably all too justified in the context of Victorian Britain. The compositors responsible for setting the text walked out when they got to the section covering the words between *C* and *Fizzle*, and the self-evident challenges to 'chastity of language' that particular entries in this section of the alphabet presented. Printing was suspended in 1890, and the existing sheets of the volume were destroyed. Farmer lost the subsequent court case against the printers.

James Murray, after long discussion in the Philological Society with reference to the *OED* (and a further exchange of letters with Farmer), decided to play safe and exclude potentially offensive words too. Yet the resulting uneasiness within the relationships of truth, history, and the art of lexicography did not pass unnoticed. As still more letters to the dictionary were quick to point out, surely such silence (even if it satisfied certain sensibilities) also meant that descriptive principles – and the real truths of both history and language – had thereby been denied. *Cunt* 'is an old English word of Teutonic origin, & is just as good English (though by the nature of things not so much used in polite society) as the words leg, arm, heart, stomack', as one writer argued, contesting its omission.

Trench's precepts on the descriptive duty of the modern lexicographer ('it is no task of the maker [of a dictionary] to select the *good* words of a language') had conspicuously been abandoned, just as they would be for, say, the lexis of contraception in the first edition of the *OED*, on which silence also conspicuously descends. Taboo words would finally be included in the *OED*'s 'inventory' almost a century later, in the *OED Supplements* edited between 1972 and 1986 by Robert Burchfield.

A conspicuous indirection in definition could elsewhere provide a way of filtering the problematic truths of usage. John Ash, a Baptist minister, did, for example, decide to include *fuck* in his own *New and Complete Dictionary of the English Language* in 1775, defining it as 'To perform the act of generation, to have to do with a woman' (he also labelled it a *low vulgar word*). *Coition* in Johnson is defined by the cryptic 'the act by which two bodies come together'; to *ravish* is 'to construpate by force'. Delicacy of a different kind attended terms such as *woman-palaver* ('illicit commerce with a woman or women') or *tribade* ('a woman who practices unnatural vice with other women') in the *OED*. As here, notions of what is 'natural' (and thereby 'right') can push definition – and attendant images of truth – in one direction or another. Morally evaluative metalanguage meanwhile serves to foreground a number of ideologically constructed images of cultural proscription. The dictionary-maker here is clearly critic as well as historian. Criticism, moreover, can involve far more than just matters of language.

Moral truth

Forms of moral authority can, as here, therefore also intervene in the kind of meanings which dictionary-makers can choose to present. *Adultery*, defined with determined objectivity in the modern *Bloomsbury English Dictionary* as 'voluntary sexual relations between a married person and somebody other than his or her spouse', is, in Johnson, 'The act of violating the bed of a married person' (a definition echoed in both the first edition of the *OED* and in Webster's work). Webster's moral stance within his dictionary can be particularly marked. Exemplary maxims for right behaviour accompany definitions for words such as *improve* and *education*. 'It is the duty, as it is the desire of a good man, to *improve* in grace and piety', Webster wrote under the former. 'To give children a good *education* in manners, arts and science, is important; to give them a religious *education* is indispensible', he advised under *education*. Being *happy* is defined in a similar way,

in an entry in which notions of truth (and true happiness) are
firmly located in Christian belief: 'The pleasurable sensations
derived from the gratification of sensual appetites render a person
temporarily *happy*; but he can only be esteemed really and
permanently *happy*, who enjoys peace of mind in the favor of God.'
Quotations from the Bible add further support. '*Happy* am I, for
the daughters will call me blessed' (Genesis, xxx); '*Happy* is that
people whose God is Jehovah' (Psalms, cxliv). *Infidel*, perhaps
predictably, is defined in rather different terms: 'One who
disbelieves the inspiration of the Scriptures, and the divine origin
of Christianity.' 'The *infidel* writer is a great enemy to society', an
illustrative citation under *infidel* affirms.

Truth in Webster's *Dictionary* is emphatically Christian truth in
ways which deliberately permeate the structures of legitimate
meaning – for both language and society. Johnson's work is
similar. As his entry for *Christmas* reveals ('The day on which the
nativity of our blessed Saviour is celebrated'), pronouns can also
emerge as an important ideological device. Here, the use of 'our'
reveals assumptions of a shared set of meanings that encompass
world as well as word, and which are equally embedded in a wide
range of other entries (*saviour*: 'redeemer: he that has saved
mankind from certain death'; *save*: 'to preserve finally from eternal
death'). Modern dictionaries tend, in contrast, to display marked
neutrality in such matters, displacing notions of meaning which
are focused exclusively through one religion (at the expense of
other co-existing forms of faith) by a determined tolerance (and
multiculturalism).

Save, as defined in the *Bloomsbury English Dictionary*, is therefore
'in some beliefs, to free someone from the consequences of sin';
salvation in the sense of 'deliverance from sin through Jesus
Christ' is given as a specific subsense, restricted to the field of
'Christianity'. Webster's definition had conversely drawn attention
to 'that firm belief of God's testimony, and of the truth of the
gospel' which *salvation* revealed. Entries for *soul* were particularly

telling. 'The immaterial and immortal spirit of man', states
Johnson. 'The spiritual, rational, and immortal substance in man,
which distinguishes him from brutes', Webster endorses with equal
certainty. 'The immortality of the soul is a fundamental article of
the Christian system', he added. Distancing formulae ('is believed
to', 'is ... regarded as') in the corresponding entry in the
Bloomsbury English Dictionary instead carefully qualify both
usage and belief: 'in some systems of religious belief, the spiritual
part of a human being that is believed to continue to exist after the
body dies. The soul is sometimes regarded as subject to future
reward and punishment, and sometimes as able to take a form that
allows it to remain on or return to earth.'

'Them' and 'us', women and men

Being 'true', as Johnson's own entry for this word confirms, is
therefore perhaps inherently problematic. If, on the one hand, it
signifies that which is 'not false, not erroneous; agreeing with fact',
on the other, it can equally be used to mean 'not false; agreeing
with our own thoughts' when who 'we' are can materially affect
what is regarded as either 'false' or 'true'. Neutrality remains
difficult, even within modern dictionaries. Questions of 'us' and
'them' are perhaps impossible to avoid.

Another divide, for example, can appear all too clearly in terms of
gender and its representation. Bilingual dictionaries, as in
Élisabeth Campbell's examination of examples used in Collins
Robert dictionaries of French and English, can be a particularly
rich source of examples. Here a *latch-key child* is, for example,
specified as 'one whose mother works' ('*enfant dont la mère
travaille*'), confirming ideological undercurrents in which a
woman's place is, by implication, still in the home (compare the
more neutral 'a child whose parents are at work'). Illustrative
examples throughout the dictionary meanwhile centre concerns of
domesticity and exhausting children for women (or, conversely,
men and professional achievement). *Lourd* ('heavy') is hence

exemplified by 'Trois enfants à élever, c'est trop lourd pour elle' ('It's too much for her to raise three children'). *Crise* (crisis) prompts the example 'elle est prise d'une crise de nettoyage', where cleaning (*nettoyage*) provides an appropriate context for the headword. *Absenter* (to be absent) brings 'elle s'absente souvent de son travail' ('she's often absent from work'), while under *air*, we are told 'elle n'avait pas l'air de vouloir travailler' ('she didn't give the impression of wanting to work'). Discourses of appearance enact other divides ('elle ne sait pas s'habiller': 'she doesn't know how to dress'), with a wide range of examples for weight, figure, and image for women. Were one to sit down and read the dictionary, a wide range of subliminal messages might well be conveyed.

Being corpus-based can, as here, merely confront us with other truths (stereotypical and otherwise) which permeate the societies in which we live. The conflicted examples found under *heave* in the 1987 *Collins Cobuild English Dictionary* (a learners' dictionary which uses full-sentence definition) provide a further useful illustration. Here, physical power and masculinity neatly interweave. *Heave* in the sense 'If you **heave** or if you **heave** something that is heavy or difficult to move, you push, pull, or lift it using a lot of effort' is supported by 'Lee heaved himself with a groan from his chair', and 'the rock was as large as a small motor car'. ' "Heave!" cried Jack.' Likewise, 'He heaved a table at me' appears as an example beneath 'If you **heave** something heavy in a particular direction, you throw it there'. *Heave* in the sense 'If something **heaves**, it moves up and down or in and out with large regular movements', however, returns us to another all too gendered stereotype: 'she was in a state of suppressed emotion: heaving breasts and short breaths'.

Still worse, as Patricia Kaye has noted, is the narrative of female instability and alcoholism which also lurks in *Cobuild*'s evidence and examples. Examples such as 'She had a drunken row with her *gigolo*'; 'she claims she's not an *alcoholic*'; 'She fought off alcoholism and *dependence* on pain-killing drugs' serve to narrate images of gender that can seem far from neutral. Age-old stories of woman as victim and woman as romantic proliferate too ('He *abandoned* her and went off to Nigeria'; 'she abandoned herself to grief'; 'Harold fell short of her idea of *romance*').

If some attempts at gender equality seem to have been made, gender-specific stereotypes can, as here, remain pervasive, both in the underlying corpus and the choices and selections made from this material. Corpora, as we have seen, simply reflect the way language is used. Dominant patterns of language can, in this light, disturbingly reflect long-engrained habits of thought. Truth here is aligned with particular patterns in cultural history, founded in particular conceptions of social space and social meaning. *Truth*: 'Conformable to fact or reality', wrote Webster, with commendable certainty: 'The *truth* of history constitutes its whole value'. Which truths are given value (and which are not) can, as we have seen, nevertheless weave a complex pattern in lexicographical practice, in both past and present history.

Chapter 6
Last words

> Truly our dictionary-makers are toilers at a Sisyphean task –
> just as soon as they have got 'Z' neatly caged an enlarged
> and adipose 'A' has broken loose at the other end of the
> menagerie.

This 1928 review of the *Oxford English Dictionary* neatly points
out the fallacy of 'last words' for any lexicographer of a living
language. The image of Sisyphus (condemned to an endless cycle in
which he must roll a boulder to the top of a hill, only to watch it
descend and begin his task once more) could, as here, seem all too
apt. Seventy years since research first began, the end of the
alphabet had, for the *OED*, indeed been reached. The fact that its
first part – *A–Ant* – had been published in 1884 (pre-dating words
such as *aeronautics* in its modern sense) or that words in C,
published in 1888–91, pre-dated *cinema* and associated forms,
nevertheless confirmed that the task now merely had to be
resumed. Throughout the alphabet, both time and language had
moved on apace.

Dictionary-makers through the ages have been forced to confront
the ways in which what they achieve is, in Samuel Johnson's
words, 'ended, but not completed'. Johnson published the first
edition of his dictionary in 1755 but continued to work on it in
various ways to the end of his life. Noah Webster's *Compendious*

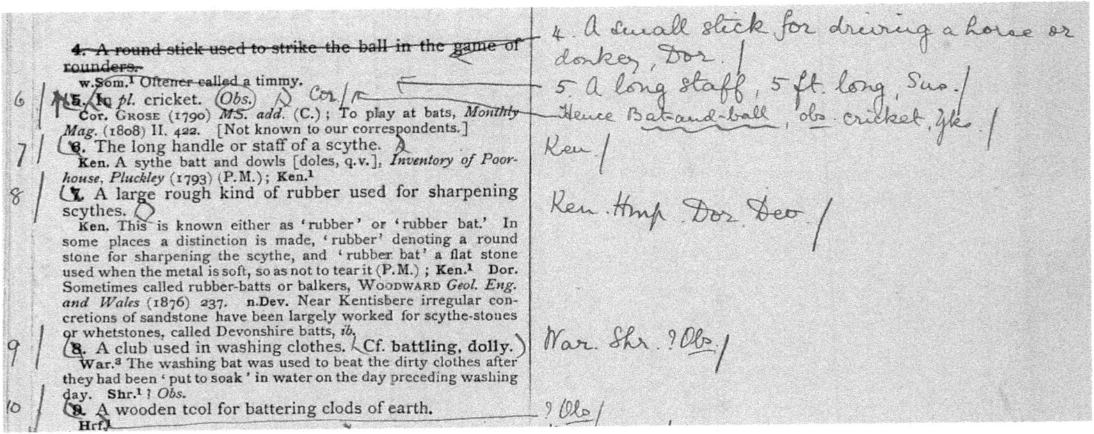

4. A round stick used to strike the ball in the game of rounders.

w.Som.¹ Otter-called a timmy.

4. pl. cricket. (Obs.) [Con./] Cor. GROSE (1790) MS. add. (C.); To play at bats, Monthly Mag. (1808) II. 422. [Not known to our correspondents.]

5. The long handle or staff of a scythe.
Ken. A sythe batt and dowls [doles, q.v.], Inventory of Poorhouse, Pluckley (1793) (P.M.); Ken.¹

6. A large rough kind of rubber used for sharpening scythes.
Ken. This is known either as 'rubber' or 'rubber bat.' In some places a distinction is made, 'rubber' denoting a round stone for sharpening the scythe, and 'rubber bat' a flat stone used when the metal is soft, so as not to tear it (P.M.); Ken.¹ Dor. Sometimes called rubber-batts or balkers, WOODWARD Geol. Eng. and Wales (1876) 237. n.Dev. Near Kentisbere irregular concretions of sandstone have been largely worked for scythe-stones or whetstones, called Devonshire batts, ib.

7. A club used in washing clothes. [Cf. batting, dolly.]
War.³ The washing bat was used to beat the dirty clothes after they had been 'put to soak' in water on the day preceding washing day. Shr.¹ Obs.

8. A wooden tool for battering clods of earth.

[Handwritten annotations:]

4. A small stick for driving a horse or donkey, Dor.

5. A long staff, 5 ft. long, Suss. Hence bat-and-ball, obs. cricket, Yks.

Ken.

Ken. Hmp. Dor. Som.

War. Shr. ? Obs.

? Obs.

[Margin numbers: 6, 7, 8, 9, 10]

15. Part of Joseph Wright's early entry for *bat* in his notebooks; the text of his *English Dialect Dictionary* has been pasted in, and Wright's careful annotations add new senses, patterns of use, and labels

Dictionary of 1806 was succeeded by his *American Dictionary* of 1828, and then by a revised edition of 1840–1. Joseph Wright completed the six volumes of his *English Dialect Dictionary* in 1905, spanning words such as *abate* (an adverb used in North Lincolnshire to mean 'accustomed to, in the habit of doing anything') to *zwodder*, an obsolete Somerset word signifying 'a drowsy, stupid state of body and mind'. If the dictionary was now formally at an end, Wright's private notebooks (illustrated in Figure 15) again tell a different story. Each page of the printed text was cut up and pasted in, and accompanied with copious annotations and additions, changes and revisions. For Wright, the dictionary had merely been halted by publication, rather than finished in any definitive sense. As Wright's notes confirm, there is always more to be said – more to be discovered about the past (and the nature of historical meaning), and always more to be said about the present, in which, as we have seen, words are never still.

Changes and challenges

While the medium and methods of dictionary-making have changed significantly across the centuries, it is nevertheless true that the physical and tactile nature of the dictionary has, until recent years, been a staple element of its identity. As in the activity of browsing the dictionary, the dictionary-user, at least traditionally, flicked through its pages to locate information, rather than using a browser in its most recent sense ('an interface between user and content in an electronic form'). 'It is the least curious of persons who can refer to a dictionary and not permit his glance to be caught by an unusual word or spelling which will lead him to browse among other equally strange words and topics', the lexicographer Robert Collison wrote, extolling the virtues of browsing in 1955, as he surveyed existing dictionaries in a range of languages. Even if 'the knowledge thus gained may be of little practical value … there is nevertheless the chance that a mind may be stimulated into exploring a fresh field of thought, or that a flagging interest may be newly revived'.

Modern dictionaries (and dictionary-making), as other chapters have explored, are in this and other respects widely affected by the digital revolution. Just as in other revolutions, here too the old order is inevitably challenged by the new. Change can prompt adaptation – or fears about obsolescence. How the dictionary is to be used (or 'accessed', in another ongoing shift of sense), as well as how it is to be written, and by whom, emerge as new areas of investigation (and potential concern). Fears that the dictionary as digital text might, in effect, spell out the last word for dictionaries in print have, moreover, frequently been mooted in recent years. Few revolutions, after all, take place without any victims whatsoever.

Print dictionaries can admittedly have significant disadvantages. Portability and usefulness often have an inverse correlation. Economies of size tend to go hand in hand with economies of content; in the compressed format of many pocket and 'mini' dictionaries, definitions are condensed, as is the wordlist. If such works are more useful in that they can be slotted into a bag or briefcase, they are correspondingly less useful since what one might desire to know might not, in fact, be contained within their pages. Larger texts can nevertheless present other problems. Desk dictionaries, for instance, are so called for a reason; the comprehensive information they contain can readily be consulted at home or work, but transporting a dictionary of this kind – having its more comprehensive information on hand as a ready point of reference – can be distinctly problematic. The American novelist Mark Twain already provided apposite illustration of this fact in 1872 in his autobiographical narrative *Roughing It*. Travelling to Nevada in an overland stagecoach, he was accompanied by his brother and an 'Unabridged Dictionary' weighing six pounds. 'Every time we avalanched from one end of the stage to another, the Unabridged Dictionary would come too; and every time ... it damaged somebody', he wrote. As here, the physical text could be a hazard rather than a help.

Even when in stasis, the wealth of information contained by such comprehensive tomes – or, still worse, by multi-volume scholarly dictionaries such as the *OED* or the Dutch *Woordenboek der Nederlandsche Taal* (which can require entire bookcases in terms of storage) – can render them distinctly cumbersome objects. Finding the requisite piece of information – and with the speed one might desire – can be challenging.

Electronic dictionaries transcend such physical constraints with ease. In this respect, the electronic sphere is a great leveller. Even the largest dictionary can (at least given sufficient time and finances) be transformed into machine-readable text; the writing of new dictionaries is, of course, digital from the beginning. The portability and omnipresence of electronic devices for many users, meanwhile, ensure that access is no longer restricted by proximity to a desk-top computer or even a lap-top. '*NOAD* to go', stated the *New Oxford American Dictionary* in 2005. The purchaser of the physical text (containing over 2,000 pages) simultaneously acquired an enclosed CD-ROM, together with a phone/PDA application, rendering information fully searchable, wherever the user might be. Further confirming the rapidity of change in this respect, the launch of the iPad in early 2010 also brought a swift lexicographic response ('Designed to make use of the best of the device's rich features, Merriam-Webster's dictionaries for iPad provide an engaging user experience that brings traditional paper-edition content to the high-resolution iPad screen', Merriam-Webster persuasively proclaimed).

Dictionaries as digital texts, moreover, no longer sit passively on a bookcase, waiting to be used. Instead, interactive features such as 'Word of the Day' (despatched electronically to your Inbox, either on a computer or mobile phone, or other mobile electronic device) proffer information on a range of words. For users in search of information, searching is electronic rather than manual. Search terms are typed into a search box and the desired information appears in response. A query is resolved in seconds, eliminating the laborious hunt for the right page and the right entry (as well as the challenges of small print) which can characterize our use of the dictionary as physical text. Searches can, moreover, be far more sophisticated – involving phrases as well as words. Some bilingual dictionaries allow users to filter searches according to the level of formality of the form required, or the part of speech. Digital dictionaries can, in addition, easily be multilingual, so that users can, from the same site, access information across a wide range of languages.

In contrast to Figure 1, a new anatomy of the dictionary entry now becomes possible, one in which, say, hypertext links allow cross-references, images, or sound files (again, in a range of languages), as well as links to other supporting material, such as encyclopaedic information which might be embedded in other works. *OED Online*, for example, links in to the *Dictionary of National Biography*, as well as the *Historical Thesaurus of English*. Interfaces are often strikingly user-friendly, and content is invitingly presented. The high cost of colour reproduction for illustrative images is also rendered irrelevant. The visual images provided can often be enlarged – enabling more detail and a literal close-up – should the user so wish.

The dictionary's adaptation to its new environment might therefore seem an unqualified success – at least for those users with access to such features. A basic computer literacy suffices to navigate the typical dictionary site. The information provided by a digital text also has the potential to be far more up to date. Here the flexibility of an online space tallies productively with the dynamism of a living language, and changing evidence on this. New words or senses, for example, can be added to online dictionaries far more easily than they can to print editions. Neither dictionary-user nor dictionary-maker need wait for a new print edition and the kind of full-scale revision throughout the alphabet which this can demand. As in the ongoing revision of *OED Online*, entries can now be added at any point across the wordlist;

new entries in June 2010 included *animal rightist* and *geoengineering*, *hotdogging* ('the action of showing off or boastfully displaying one's abilities or accomplishments'), and *microinvasive* ('invasive at a microscopic level'). Additional 'feminizations' – such as *la pasteure* (a female pastor) and *sénetrice* (a female senator) – were likewise incorporated into the *Oxford Languages Dictionary Online* site in November 2010. *Maire* (mayor) at the same time became a female as well as a male noun.

The sheer diversity and range of lexicographic material available on the World Wide Web can nevertheless reveal areas of potential concern – especially for dictionary publishers. Print dictionaries of course need to be purchased, or consulted in the reference section of a library. Open-access digital dictionaries – a common phenomenon on the Web – conversely seem to offer an attractive democracy of knowledge. No purchase needs to be made; information on word meaning is proffered entirely free of charge, accessible wherever the user might happen to be, as long as they have an Internet connection. The dictionary is removed from individual ownership, or even from the need to pay a subscription to access the material provided. '*Wiktionary* – the **free** dictionary', as its website proclaims. *Dictionary.com* promises 'The largest and most trusted free online dictionary', here on a site which currently has over 50 million visitors a month. Precisely like commercially published dictionaries, the latter, for instance, proclaims its status in terms of authority and reliability ('the world's largest and most authoritative online dictionary' which 'provides reliable access to millions of word definitions, spelling, audio pronunciations'). Unlike current commercially published dictionaries, however, as its website is also at pains to stress, full access to all features comes entirely without cost.

The range of free information about words and word meanings available on the Web is striking. Simply typing the word about which one desires to know more, together with the word 'definition', into the search box of a search engine, will produce a swift set of responses, from a range of sites. A search for *unfriend* (a form voted 'Word of the Year' by Oxford Dictionaries in 2009) produces, for instance, around 10,900 results in 0.26 seconds. While not all the information thereby elicited will be equally useful (and some may in fact be precisely the opposite), doubts can nevertheless emerge about future levels of need for commercial dictionaries, especially among general users. If material can be obtained without financial cost, why should users buy particular dictionaries, either in print or (via subscription) in an online form?

The promises made by websites such as *YourDictionary.com* to provide 'the last word in words' can, in this light, seem a threat to dictionaries as well as an intended guarantee of comprehensiveness. 'Internet blamed as Chambers hit by death of dictionary', as an alarming headline in December 2009 announced. As subsequent discussion made plain, it was the 'digital revolution' that was identified as the cause of 'a decline in sales of dictionaries'. The Chambers offices in Scotland, founded in 1819, were to be closed. A spokesman for Hachette UK (the current owners of Chambers dictionaries) was explicit on the dangers that dictionaries and dictionary-making could now face: 'The digital revolution is changing the ways readers consume news and search for information. People are moving away from printed reference books and going online where, generally, they expect to get their information for free.'

Dictionary-making redefined?

The fact that, in a further exercise of democracy, one can, moreover, bypass the dictionary-maker altogether and simply craft one's own entry using sites such as *Wiktionary* or *Urban Dictionary* ('the dictionary **you wrote**', as its home page affirms) presents still other concerns in this context. If dictionaries can be written by users and for users, is the dictionary-maker too potentially rendered obsolescent? Websites such as those for *Urban Dictionary* and *Wiktionary*, for example, offer what is known as 'bottom-up lexicography', placing ordinary speakers and writers at the core of the ways in which the dictionaries in question are to be made. The definitions of dictionary-making which such sites present can be particularly telling. *Lexicography*: 'The art of making a dictionary. Anyone who adds to urbandictionary.com [*sic*] is a lexicographer', a post on *Urban Dictionary* proclaims. 'I have just spent an hour lexicographing in the urban dictionary' states the accompanying example.

'One who writes or compiles a dictionary', the corresponding definition on *Wiktionary* affirms. As its name suggests, *Wiktionary* offers a blend of 'wiki' ('a collaborative website which can be directly edited using only a web browser, often by anyone with access to it') with the kind of interpretative structures that have long characterized traditional dictionaries. 'Compiling and writing' for dictionary-makers in this domain is nevertheless rather different. Rather than a collaborative venture between co-editors or assistants in a dictionary office or within a professional team, it is based in the activities of an online community which anyone, in principle, can join. On *Wiktionary*, volunteers and users can write entries or add information, update existing forms, and change the data that other users have already placed online. The 'Collaborative International Dictionary of English' (which is, in fact, based on a 1913 text of Webster's *Dictionary*) offers opportunities similar in kind.

While collaboration in various guises has, as we have seen, a long history in lexicography, domains such as these clearly exceed the kind of collaborative potential which we early saw at work in Baret's *Alvearie* or even the *OED*. Baret's readers, as we saw in Chapter 2, were also invited to add words and meanings under appropriate headings as they saw fit. 'We do but follow the example of the Grimms, when we call upon Englishmen to come forward and write their own Dictionary for themselves', the original *Proposal* for the *OED* likewise proclaimed in 1860. For the first edition of the *OED*, volunteers not only read books for relevant quotations but could, in fact, also become subeditors, sorting the assembled information and providing preliminary classifications into possible senses and sense divisions. Other volunteers could, if they possessed sufficient expertise, become critical readers, commenting on drafts of the text, suggesting improvements, or spotting inconsistencies. As Figure 16 illustrates, volunteer endeavour can still remain important.

16. **Ongoing collaborative endeavours: appealing for new readers, and new quotations, for the *Oxford English Dictionary***

Volunteers did not, however, actually write the dictionary nor did those who, in Germany, participated in the gathering of material for the *Deutsches Wörterbuch*. Collaborative online dictionaries therefore collapse this distinction; a 'lexicographer', as in the definitions discussed above, can – at least on one level – be anyone who chooses to write or add to a dictionary entry (irrespective of the presence or absence of knowledge about language and language structures, or the kind of professional training and relevant qualifications they might – or might not – have). Speaking a language is deemed qualification enough, as is sometimes simply having an opinion about a given word or usage. Modern dictionaries can thereby move from being exclusive 'in-house' publications to dynamic virtual texts which exist as strikingly inclusive enterprises.

Examining the entry for *unfriend* on *Urban Dictionary* reveals therefore a range of voices, rather than the seamless anonymity which characterizes the modern professional dictionary text. Meaning has clearly been configured by different users; defining styles proliferate. As different posts proclaim, *unfriend* can be 'The opposite of befriending someone. When you unfriend someone you don't necessarily become their enemy per say [*sic*], but you are no longer their friend', or it can be pithily defined as 'a coward's way of conflict management in the world of social networking'. It can be 'the action of removing someone from your friends list on any social network' – or, in another variation on a common theme, here with a strong sense of personal animus (which would likewise be out of place in modern professional lexicography), it is:

> The act of removing people from your 'friends list' on Live Journal
> just to let them know you hate them, and you hope they die. In fact,
> you don't just hate them and hope that they die, but you hope they
> die a long, slow, painful, gut wrenching death. Preferably in a
> Turkish Prison that is overrun with skin eating mutant leeches.

A wide range of other competing and similar propositions appear under the same heading, accompanied by a correspondingly diverse set of sample sentences which, idiomatically, illustrate usage: 'I shouldn't have agreed to her friend request, so I'm just going to unfriend her'; 'I am unfriending you because of what you did today, I feel you can no longer be my friend.' If the dictionary-maker of the traditional dictionary text imposes order (as indeed in Guy Miège's description of the dictionary as 'language orderly digested' with which we ended Chapter 1), the digital dictionary-maker on *Urban Dictionary* will instead tend to engage with individual elements of individual entries. Definitions and examples are not posted in a process of systematic engagement with a particular set of words or alphabetic sequence; an overview – either of the dictionary or the individual entry – is not attempted.

If order is, on one level, imposed through the fact of alphabetic arrangement, it can nevertheless be absent, at least in a strictly lexicographic sense, within the entries themselves. Entries, for instance, are split not into carefully differentiated and distinct senses, but instead present a numbered series of 'posts' – a collectivity of individual contributions in which overlap, conflict, and dissent are all common. Thirty posts appear under *chat*, for instance, variously and variably encompassing its use as a noun, adjective, verb, as well as offering translations in which *chat* is seen as part of another language altogether ('This is the French for cat'). Meanings range, in no particular order, across 'a person very un-attractive', 'to engage in small talk', 'have a word', 'a slang form for flea', and 'something utterly rank' (among others).

Entry length and contents are also markedly variable. Posts under *alternative* range from over 20 lines of definition/description to brief one-liners; entries (as in those cited for *lexicography* or *unfriend*) can lack spell-checking or proof-reading in ways that resoundingly confirm the spontaneity and immediacy of what is recorded. Neutrality can also deliberately be abandoned; meaning can be personal, reflecting hates and preferences, or even prejudices. Sexism and racism can be explicit.

Even if the prototypical binary structure of the dictionary entry has been maintained, what is valued can therefore be the transgressive or subversive – reflecting patterns of meaning which can often challenge the established versions of conventional dictionary texts. Shared sympathies and opinions – rather than a shared basis in facts – deliberately render *Urban Dictionary* a very different experience. Attitudes to school, sex, friendship, politics, or appearance form recurrent ways in which the users of *Urban Dictionary* can and do choose to 'define their world', as the website's slogan affirms.

The notion of meaning as established through a systematic examination of the dominant patterns of use is usually remote. A word such as *school* is therefore defined not in terms of its objective role as an institution which delivers learning in various ways, but as 'A place where everyone secretly hates each other including students, staff and teachers and is a nightmare'. With over 4,700 positive ratings (signalled by an affirmatory thumbs-up on the screen), this has been firmly endorsed by *Urban Dictionary*'s online community. 'A place where young, innocent defenceless children are kept prisoner and forced to learn useless stuff like algebra', another popular definition explains. 'School sucks' states an illustrative example, pithily invented for the occasion rather than being derived from a database of evidence.

The entries on *Urban Dictionary*, of course, in such ways usefully remind us of the authored nature of the dictionary text (which, in other circumstances, we might be tempted to forget). We are nevertheless in some ways presented with a paradox. The modernity of *Urban Dictionary* (and similar sites) is undoubted; lexicography of this kind would have been impossible in a pre-digital age and without an online community. In other respects, however, we can find ourselves simply returned once more to the past – to an era before the emergence of professional lexicography (with its strongly empiricist basis), as well as to patterns of definition (and a dominant subjectivity) which mainstream lexicography has long abandoned.

Such affinities can be surprising. Definitions in the 18th century – as indeed in Johnson's own work – could, for example, clearly choose to privilege the personal and opinionated, rather than the neutral and objective, the scientific and empirical. The narrative of Johnson's conflicted relationship with his patron Lord Chesterfield is densely embedded in his dictionary under entries such as *patron* ('commonly a wretch who supports with insolence, and is paid with flattery'), *dedication* ('a servile address to a patron'), or *gratefulness* ('duty to benefactors. Now obsolete'). Narratives on faith and morality, or attitudes to gender, can be equally pervasive.

Like those of *Urban Dictionary*, Johnson's entries too could reveal the pull of language attitudes. Johnson's dislike for the newer meaning of *immaterial* (as 'unimportant; without weight') can, for instance, neatly be paralleled by posted definitions for *decimate* on *Urban Dictionary*. While Johnson proscribes the former, allowing personal response to govern the presentation of information on meaning and use ('This sense has crept into the conversation and writings of barbarians; but ought to be utterly rejected'), posts on *decimate* conspicuously embrace the kind of etymological fallacy (discussed in Chapter 4) that modern descriptive dictionary practice has shed. 'A frequently misused word', the first definition on *Urban Dictionary* states: 'Decimate literally means to reduce something by a tenth but many people use it instead to mean "totally destroy". The word "obliterate" would be a better choice than "decimate"'. Etymology (and a Latin root which, as in *decimal*, signifies a tenth or pertaining to tenths) are preferentially set against language practice. The

Oxford English Corpus, meanwhile, records the overwhelming
dominance of the meaning which is here condemned.

Rather than redefining the dictionary-maker, the digital text
can, as here, in some ways simply reappropriate features of a much
earlier model. Metaphorically, we arrive at a state in which old
wine – the kind of disregard for evidence that could characterize
the prescriptive tradition – is placed in strikingly new bottles (the
digital environment, and the actions of an online community).

Diversity and the digital text

Urban Dictionary is part of a spectrum of dictionary texts which
make up modern lexicography. It is, however, determinedly non-
representative in both evidence and inclusion. Even its interest in
slang and the vigorously colloquial is very different from the kind
of rigour – and systematic examination – which modern
professional dictionaries of slang habitually reveal.

Dictionaries, as Samuel Johnson wrote a few months before he
died, are 'like watches. The worst is better than none, but even
the best cannot be expected to go quite true.' Written long
before the advent of the digital revolution, Johnson's words
remain important, raising the difference between dictionary
and dictionary, between worse and better. As in Chapter 1,
while our modern idioms still refer to an illusory 'the dictionary',
the question of which dictionary is to be used will, in this
context too, also make a significant difference. Even in 1998,
over 400 online dictionaries for English alone existed on the
Web. Figures are now far higher. Comparing like with like
(or, more significantly, like with unlike) can nevertheless
be difficult.

Wiktionary and *Urban Dictionary*, for example – even if both
produced by online communities – are strikingly different in tone
and style (as well as in what they intend to achieve). Entry templates

in *Wiktionary* aim to clarify the desired format for the information which individuals might choose to give, while its community portal provides an 'Information desk', a 'tea-room' (for questions concerning particular words), and other virtual locations such as the 'etymology scriptorium' (for discussion about word origin). An equally virtual 'beer parlour' provides a space for 'policy discussion and cross-entry discussion'. Interaction between users – the suggestion of additional senses, the provision of more information, or posts that contest what has been written – can here genuinely reinforce the sense of a collaborative project, as well as the sense of a real and wide-ranging interest in words and meanings.

Sense divisions are numbered, reflecting the intentional distinction of different shades of meaning (rather than the kind of semantic cacophony with which users of *Urban Dictionary* can be presented). Accompanying examples also tend to avoid personal bias or opinion. Instead, in line with common lexicographic practice, they can strive to embed the word in question in a 'representative' sample of ordinary usage (as in 'Our children attend a public school in our neighbourhood', here illustrating the US or Canadian use of *school* to mean 'An institution dedicated to teaching and learning; an educational institution'). A separate UK sense ('An educational institution providing primary and secondary education, prior to tertiary education') is also provided. Dated and attributed quotations on the model of professional lexicography can also be used (though none, in fact, appear under *school*). Grammatical information and, as above, information on regional distribution and currency, can usefully be included.

While a commitment to quality control (and to careful moderation) move *Wiktionary* closer to the kind of consistency of presentation we might expect in a modern professional text, inevitable differences remain. Contextual information and examples can be present in some entries, absent in others. Entry templates can be followed in narrower or looser ways. Likewise, sense elaboration can be extensive or minimal, depending on the entry consulted. Invented examples, rather than the calibrated evidence of a corpus, moreover, lack empirical validity – and true representativeness. How authoritative – and indeed accurate – individual entries are will also vary; information is, after all, not derived from the kind of research into collocation and frequency on which the modern professional dictionary typically depends. Like other online texts of this kind, *Wiktionary* is inevitably a work in progress – one being crafted by a strikingly diverse group of dictionary-makers across the world, united not by professional commitment but by an enduring interest in the ways in which language can be probed in terms of use and meaning.

The proliferation of free online dictionaries offers another form in which dictionary-making has adapted to the digital world. It testifies too to the ongoing popularity of the dictionary as resource in a variety of languages. Diversity here can, however, be striking, and perhaps bewildering. Some dictionaries are 'closed'. Based on digitized versions of earlier (sometimes, much earlier) printed editions, they offer rapid access to a range of definitions. Johnson's metaphor of the dictionary as watch, however, can usefully urge caution here too. *Dictionary.net*, for instance, offers a range of definitions derived from other works, including Bierce's *Devil's Dictionary* of 1911, together with a 1913 edition of Webster's *Revised Unabridged Dictionary*. Encyclopaedic sources such as the 'CIA World Factbook 2002' are also included. Even when placed on a 21st-century website, lexicographical time here is clearly running slow. Neither Bierce nor the 1913 Webster are representative of language as used today (the inclusion of entries from other 'bottom-up' works such as *The Collaborative International Dictionary of English* can intentionally act as a corrective, though potentially raising problems of a different kind).

Wordnik (another popular free dictionary site) conversely embeds entries from much earlier texts such the 19th-century *Century Dictionary*, or (again) the 1913 edition of Webster, as well as an edition of the *American Heritage Dictionary* and *Wiktionary*, while also making use of a 'corpus' of billions of words that provide samples of current use in both speech and writing. Additional text boxes meanwhile provide the facility for any word to be translated into over 50 languages. Functionality on such sites (in another new aspect of dictionary metalanguage) can nevertheless be limited when compared with modern professional equivalents. Translations, for example, cannot be calibrated by style or part of speech. Recent changes in language, moreover, habitually remain without the kind of quantitative underpinning and research that characterize commercial sites, potentially leading to a proliferation of *ad hoc* coinages among new entries rather than revealing the systematic documentation of language as it exists in wider use. The level of ordinary engagement and interaction that sites such as *Wordnik* foster can nevertheless be attractive; one can easily add comments to different entries, interacting with other users in an ongoing exchange of opinion and advice.

Professional dictionaries, meanwhile, have their own sites. Merriam-Webster's is a hive of activity in ways which far surpasses Baret's *Alvearie*. Advertisements (both static and moving) distractingly frame the page, while a search box invites the potential user to search a range of reference texts. The word of the day (for 5 August 2010), we are told, is *colloquy*, a word provided with two senses, an example sentence, a sound file, as well as a discursive etymology. A list of 'top 10' words offers other information: for example, that *philtrum* – the 'vertical groove on the median line of the upper lip' – is specified as one of the 'Top 10 Words for Things You Didn't Know'. All this is free. Payment (either monthly or annually) must, however, be made to access the advertising-free 'premium services' of the *Unabridged Dictionary* and its 470,000 entries. As here, sample entries act as tasters; the detailed and clearly structured entry for *colloquy*, for example, provides not only information but acts as testimony to the quality of the commodity which subscribers can access – and in which, we are told 'the dictionary is just the beginning of the 'ultimate unabridged experience'. Using the (free) search box meanwhile provides truncated information and still more advertising. Only the payment of a subscription grants freedom from such intrusiveness, allowing users behind the paywall which prohibits full access to the most recent editions and information.

Paradoxically, on this level at least, one must pay to have less (even if one will, of course, also gain in terms of the kind of content which truly belongs to a dictionary). Such strategies are a familiar presence on the Web. Advertising subsidizes the provision of free content, while different dictionary publishers proclaim their own advertising strategies ('the web's favourite learner dictionaries', 'the first and last word in dictionaries'). The World Wide Web hence becomes a valuable, if highly competitive, marketplace; commercial dictionaries raise brand awareness, display their wares, offer free samples (Longman, for instance, offers a fully searchable text for its *Longman Dictionary of Contemporary English*), and hope that users are tempted to commit to the purchase of the additional features or texts on offer. 'Welcome to CollinsLanguage.com', as the Collins website announces: 'here you can buy downloadable dictionary software and online subscriptions to the best language resources'. If the site provides a free dictionary, this is self-evidently less extensive (and less up to date) than those available for purchase.

The dictionary as commodity

Free dictionaries proffer what is, in essence, a 'one size fits all' commodity. Professional publishing houses here excel in the opposite direction. Rather than a single free dictionary, a wide array of different texts can be presented on commercial dictionary sites – dictionaries for children (primary, junior, students), for learners of all levels in a range of different languages, for readers who require different levels of detail, and in different combinations of languages and sizes. In a sphere often dominated by the new and innovatory, it swiftly becomes clear that tradition and experience can also be prime virtues – and not least in terms of the kind of work which, as we have seen over the course of this volume, is often securely informed by qualities such as trustworthiness, authoritativeness, and reliability. The value of these associations should not be underestimated. Collins, for example, can boast of over '175 years of dictionary publishing'. Merriam-Webster's long-established reputation for high-quality reference books is similarly important. Like 'Oxford', dictionaries themselves are often seen as brands – commodities that can trade effectively on their established reputations.

It is, of course, for such reasons that traditional dictionary publishing (if now digital as well as print) continues to compete successfully against cost-free rivals. Buying a particular dictionary (or dictionary product) signifies equally an investment – emotional and intellectual – in what is provided. And, as in Johnson's metaphor of the watch, what is provided by traditional dictionary publishers is usually, of course, qualitatively different – based on ongoing research programmes, carefully balanced and up-to-date corpora (and equally up-to-date revisions), and empirical and objective (and first-hand) analysis of how language is used. Even if no dictionary can ever be quite 'true' – language is constantly changing, the dictionary-maker will always follow behind – authoritativeness is, as we have seen, the foundation of good lexicography. Fundamentally, a dictionary, whether online or in print, can only be as good as the data it contains (and the research programmes and scholarly investigation on which it rests).

What is abundantly clear in terms of the ongoing history of dictionaries and dictionary-making is the way in which a form that began, as we have seen, on clay tablets over 3,000 years ago is triumphantly continuing to adapt and to evolve – capitalizing on new environments (mobile phones, iPads, iPods), as well as on the capacity to interact with users (and for users to interact with dictionaries) in ways which clearly extend what had earlier been possible. 'Add your word to our record of English as it used today; enriched by speakers around the world, driven by the speed of technology, powered by the globalisation of language', as Macmillans proclaims of the 'Open Dictionary' facility on its website. 'Add a-Word', urges the *Macquarie Dictionary* website ('if you have come across a word or phrase that you think should be in the dictionary, you can send it to Macquarie Dictionary for consideration').

The diction of empowerment or active language learning can be prominent. No longer a gatekeeper (or border guard), the dictionary becomes a 'gateway' to improved language use. As a range of websites promise, the dictionary is a tool and a resource, a teacher and a guide in ways which likewise serve to extend Cawdrey's earlier promise, in the very first monolingual English dictionary, to offer guidance and proficiency to the 'unskilful'. Features such as 'fuzzy searching' (impossible in a print dictionary) are, for example, of particular value here, especially to language learners. The wealth of websites that engage with words and meanings likewise offers abundant proof of the ongoing interest in language, and the vitality and dynamism of dictionaries of all kinds.

The demise of print dictionaries, while often foretold, also therefore remains unrealized. Instead, paper dictionaries (with or without extra Internet links or other forms of electronic access and subscription) continue to be both published and purchased. If *browsing*, as we have seen, has come to mean consulting information on a database as well as glancing through a book in a casual and relaxed (if occasionally haphazard) way, the latter, as user-surveys reveal, is in fact often still valued by those who use a dictionary. Sometimes, scanning a page using one's eyes can in fact be preferable. Even if one can scan a list of words electronically, the information under each headword can be accessed only by clicking on it. Here, old-style paper dictionaries can paradoxically be faster – and, as users point out, far more user-friendly.

Rather than loss and displacement, it is an ongoing narrative of print and digital co-existence which, at least for the moment, seems key. Dictionaries are, in fact, far more visible than ever before – embedded in word-processing packages, and e-readers, and readily accessed by phone, print, or computer. The fact that e-readers allow users to access explanations of words while actually in the midst of reading might, of course, ultimately prove one of the most significant changes to the dictionary in print form. New avenues for dictionaries continue to appear. Recently introduced i-Phone applications for endangered languages, providing 'speaking dictionaries' for languages such as Tuvan (a minority language spoken in Tuva in Russia), reveal the ways in which technology, innovation, and the art of lexicography continue to interact. New words and senses, meanwhile, proliferate (words such as *mwah* and *noob*, *staycation* and *ecotarian* were among 267 words added to *Collins English Dictionary* in 2009). *Stab vest* (US *stab jacket*) was added to the digital version of *Macmillan's English Dictionary* in August 2010, testimony to other changes in language and society; 'Goodbye petabytes, hello zettabytes', the *Guardian* announced a few months earlier, commenting that the 'unprecedented amount of digital information' has introduced yet another new word. Dictionary-makers simply take note and adjust entries and evidence accordingly.

References and further reading

Brian Atkins and Sue Rundell, *The Oxford Guide to Practical Lexicography* (Oxford: Oxford University Press, 2008).

Henri Béjoint, *Modern Lexicography: An Introduction* (Oxford: Oxford University Press, 2000).

Henri Béjoint, *The Lexicography of English* (Oxford: Oxford University Press, 2010).

É. Campbell, 'La représentation des femmes dans les dictionnaires bilingues', *French Studies* 58 (2004): 61–76.

Anthony Cowie, *The Oxford History of English Lexicography*, 2 vols. (Oxford: Oxford University Press, 2009).

Thierry Fontanelle, *Practical Lexicography: A Reader* (Oxford: Oxford University Press, 2008).

Jonathon Green, *Chasing the Sun: Dictionary-Makers and the Dictionaries They Made* (London: Jonathan Cape, 1996).

James Hulbert, *Dictionaries: British and American* (London: Andre Deutsch, 1955).

Howard Jackson, *Lexicography: An Introduction* (London: Routledge, 2002).

Patricia Kaye, '"Women Are Alcoholics and Drug Addicts", says Dictionary', *ELT Journal* 43 (1989): 192–5.

Sidney Landau, *Dictionaries – The Art and Craft of Lexicography*, 2nd edn. (Cambridge: Cambridge University Press, 2001).

William Meijs, 'Linguistic Corpora and Lexicography', *Annual Review of Applied Linguistics* 16 (1996): 99–114.

H. Morton, *The Story of Webster's Third: Philip Gove's Controversial Dictionary and its Critics* (Cambridge: Cambridge University Press, 1994).

Lynda Mugglestone, *Lexicography and the OED: Pioneers in the Untrodden Forest* (Oxford: Oxford University Press, 2002).

Lynda Mugglestone, *Lost For Words: The Hidden History of the Oxford English Dictionary* (London and New York: Yale University Press, 2005).

Lynda Mugglestone, '"The Indefinable Something": Taboo and the English Dictionary', in *Rude Britannia*, ed. M. Gorji (London: Routledge, 2007), pp. 22–32.

Lynda Mugglestone, 'Registering the Language – Dictionaries, Diction, and the Art of Elocution', in *Eighteenth-Century English: Ideology and Change*, ed. Raymond Hickey (Cambridge: Cambridge University Press, 2010), pp. 309–38.

K. M. Elisabeth Murray, *Caught in the Web of Words: James Murray and the Oxford English Dictionary* (London and New York: Yale University Press, 1977).

Vincent Ooi, *Computer Corpus Lexicography* (Edinburgh: Edinburgh University Press, 1998).

Derek Peterson, 'Colonizing Language? Missionaries and Gikuyu Dictionaries, 1904 and 1914', *History in Africa* 24 (1997): 257–72.

Bill Ramson, *Lexical Images: The Story of the Australian National Dictionary* (Oxford: Oxford University Press, 2002).

Allen Reddick, *The Making of Johnson's Dictionary 1746–1773*, revised edn. (Cambridge: Cambridge University Press, 1996).

Ammon Shea, *Reading the Oxford English Dictionary: One Man, One Year, 21,730 Pages* (London: Penguin, 2008).

John Sinclair (ed.), *Looking Up: An Account of the COBUILD Project in Lexical Computing* (London and Glasgow: HarperCollins, 1987).

James Sledd and Wilma Ebbitt, *Dictionaries and* That *Dictionary: A Casebook on the Aims of Lexicographers and the Targets of Reviewers* (Chicago: Scott, 1962).

Bo Svensén, *A Handbook of Lexicography: The Theory and Practice of Dictionary-Making* (Cambridge: Cambridge University Press, 2009).

Richard Chenevix Trench, *On Some Deficiencies in Our English Dictionaries* (1860). Available at http://ezproxy.ouls.ox.ac.uk:2118/archive/paper-deficiencies/

Peter Trudgill, 'Standard English: What It Isn't', in *Standard English: The Widening Debate*, ed. Tony Bex and Richard Watts (London: Routledge, 1999), pp. 117–28.

Index

Index

Dictionaries

Expand your collection of
VERY SHORT INTRODUCTIONS